The Way Was Through Woods
The Story of Tomo-chi-chi

Tomo-chi-chi and Toonahawi. Cordray-Foltz photo collection.

The Way Was Through Woods

THE STORY OF TOMO-CHI-CHI

by Sara H. Banks

A Talking Leaves Book
ROBERTS RINEHART PUBLISHERS

In loving memory of Edward Cooper

The little owls cry out their legendary names,
whom I have cherished.

Contents

Chapter One   1
Chapter Two   8
Chapter Three   14
Chapter Four   21
Chapter Five   24
Chapter Six   29
Chapter Seven   32
Chapter Eight   38
Chapter Nine   44
Chapter Ten   49
Chapter Eleven   53
Chapter Twelve   58
Chapter Thirteen   63
Chapter Fourteen   69
Chapter Fifteen   74
Chapter Sixteen   77
Afterword   83
Bibliography   85

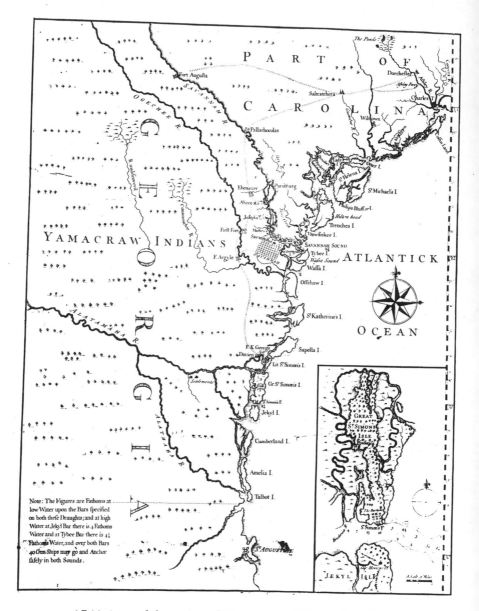

1741 map of the coast of Georgia and South Carolina.
Courtesy of the Georgia Historical Society.

After a great while, there arose a wind from the east
that gradually drove the fog from the land. The
group of people who first saw clearly the land and
the various objects of nature, now rendered visible
in the dissipating fog, were given the name of
the Wind Clan.

—John Swanton

Chapter One

In THE MIDDLE OF THE DEEP WOODS, THERE
was a clearing where deer came to feed. And there, Tomo-
chi-chi waited in the shadow of a giant oak. Motionless
and silent, he seemed nearly invisible, his deerskin leggings
blending with the colors of the forest. He was twelve years
old, tall for his age, the muscles of his bare chest already
strong. Over one shoulder he wore a quiver of arrows on
which was painted the symbol of his clan, the Wind Clan
of the Creek.

Tomo-chi-chi listened intently. His hearing was acute; he
heard the secret sounds of the forest. Not just birdsong but
the separate song of each bird; the delicate flutings of the red-
bird, the deep cooing of the passenger pigeon, and the clear
trill of the mockingbird, the "bird of a thousand tongues." He
also heard the murmur of Long Man the River, as it flowed
near his village of Coweta. In the pearly morning, while mists
from the river drifted like smoke into the branches of the
trees, he heard the faint rustle of deer as they approached.

The doe came first, her delicate hoofs barely touching the earth. She was followed closely by another female. Then, a moment later, the buck showed. He was young, his antlers still furred with velvet. Heads bowed, they ate quickly, delicate ears quivering. Tomo-chi-chi watched them, his breath shallow, his body perfectly still. He had not come to hunt, but merely to watch. He'd discovered their feeding place, thick with fallen acorns now in autumn, one day when he'd returned from fishing on the nearby Chattahoochee River. He enjoyed fishing and hunting with his friends, but sometimes he liked being alone, learning the secret ways of the woods.

An acorn fell, the tiny sound sharp in the still air. The buck lifted his head, then gave a thin whistle, and with one accord the three deer bounded back into the forest and disappeared. A moment later, Tomo-chi-chi slipped into the woods, his bare feet making no sound on the earth. Today was the beginning of the *puskita*, the Green Corn Festival, the most important celebration in the Creek year. Many visitors would be coming to Coweta from various Creek towns and villages in the Lower Creek Nation. Tomo-chi-chi was looking forward to the games and ceremonies that would take place over the next week. If he hurried, he could be at the *chungke* yard early, and get in a few throws of the spear for practice.

In 1662, Tomo-chi-chi's Creek Indian world was unspoiled and beautiful. Coweta, built along the banks of the wide Chattahoochee River, was one of the leading towns in the Creek Nation of more than fifty towns belonging to the Creek Confederacy. The Creeks lived in an area that stretched from the Alabama River on the west to the Ogeechee River on the east. The Nation was divided into two parts: the Upper Creeks lived along the Coosa, Talapoosa and Alabama Rivers, and the Lower Creeks along both banks of the Chattahoochee and in the lower coastal areas. War leaders came from "red" towns and principal chiefs from "white" or "peace" towns. Coweta was a "peace" town. Tomo-chi-chi's clan, the Wind Clan, was one of several clans belonging to that town. White for the Creeks meant that which is old, established, and united. Other villages had clans within them designated as "red," the color of danger, war, conflict, and fear. The villages and clans of the same color were called "chiefdoms." Belonging to a certain clan meant "being from the same fire," and a person from a chiefdom of one's own fire was known as "friend" (*anhissi*). Old Brim, the chief *mico* of the Lower Creek Nation, lived at Coweta and was kin to Tomo-chi-chi.

The rising sun spattered the leaves with gold as he made his way back to the village. There was much excitement as visitors arrived on foot and on horseback. In early morning, sweetly scented woodsmoke hung in the air, drifting from the chimneys of the houses and small campfires. The village was built around a plaza in which were three major structures: the *tcokofa* or town house, a summer council house, and the long, smooth boundaries of the *chungke* yard. The town house, which sat on a rise in the center of the plaza, was two stories high. Built of logs, it could hold up to 300 people. Individual houses at the edge of the plaza were built of fragrant sassafras wood, called *wisso*. Tomo-chi-chi's house was such a house and had been built by his father for his mother.

In the center of the plaza, in front of the town house, the sacred fire had been laid in preparation for the ceremony when new fires would be kindled. The Indian belief system was expressed in every phase of their lives. Their social system was enriched with ceremony. Rekindling the sacred fires each year was a symbol of purity and balance with the natural and spiritual world. Fire was considered the earthly representative of the sun, and was never extinguished with water except for funerary ceremonies when the act represented death. Fire itself was the ultimate symbol of the struggle against pollution. The Southeastern

Indians believed that when people disobeyed rules because of human frailty, the sacred fire grew polluted over time. Rekindling it was a new beginning each year. Smoke, because of its association with fire, was also important in ceremonies. The smoke of sacred tobacco was used in rituals. Puffs of smoke from sacred pipes were blown in the four cardinal directions of the earth, and bits of tobacco leaf were used in the same way, sprinkled on a fire or tossed into the air.

Tomo-chi-chi walked past the gardens and fields on the outskirts of the village. His people were an agricultural, hunting people. They fished, planted crops, tilled the soil and gleaned the wealth of wild plants and herbs of the forests, making medicines and potions. Corn was planted on mounds with bean vines climbing the cornstalks for support. Squash grew thickly at the base of the stalk. These were the "three sisters" that were the mainstay of the Creek diet. Sweet potatoes were stored in mounds near the corn cribs, while in nearby fields were also planted tobacco, pumpkins, melons, and onions. The sun touched the bright heads of the sunflowers that grew along the edges of the fields. Later in the day, old women would sit on raised platforms in the fields, "scaring" crows that flew too low over the crops.

Many people, both villagers and visitors, had already gathered at the town house. Some would stay there, others would stay with family or friends. At the *chungke* yard, Tomo-chi-chi paused to see if any of his friends had arrived. He saw many visitors, but none of his friends. It was a good day for the games, mild and fair with blue skies. The *chungke* yard had been cleared and smoothed. Surrounded by a low wall, at the center of the playing field was a pole 30 to 40 feet high. A heavy discus made of quartz waited to be rolled along the flat, sandy area.

Tomo-chi-chi removed one of the long, pointed spears from the stack in one corner of the yard. Testing it for weight, he hefted it high, then began running along the yard's edge. Taller than his friends, he was also stronger and faster. His heavy braids lashed out and the muscles of his back rippled as he threw the spear with a mighty heave. The spear landed in the earth, quivering lightly. If the discus had been rolling, he'd have stopped it. *I'll win later,* he thought, *even against the visitors.* He loved playing *chungke*.

Replacing the spear, Tomo-chi-chi realized that he was hungry. He hurried towards his mother's cabin, which was called a *huti*. His mother would be cooking *sa fji (sofkee)*, a cornmeal dish much like grits, and fresh fish. The night before, he had gone fishing with some of his friends. Sometimes they fished using hooks made of bone and lines of twisted grass fibers. Last night, they had gathered at the edge of the river and lighting torches of pitch pine, had rowed out in canoes just past the shallows. The water was as clear as glass. There, attracted by the moving lights of the torches, the sunfish appeared like silver arrowheads in the dark waters. He had caught enough fish for breakfast for his entire family, keeping them fresh in a basket sunk at the water's edge.

He loved to hunt and fish. In his deerskin quiver, he carried a blowgun and small, slender arrows feathered with thistle wool. These he used for small game. For larger game, he used a bow and arrow. The Creeks were famous arrowmakers and Tomo-chi-chi had learned to carve arrowheads from pure crystal, jasper, and quartz.

Entering his mother's *huti*, he paused in the doorway until his eyes grew accustomed to the shadowy room. His father had built the house, but according to Creek custom it belonged to his mother.

Their winter house was made of *wisso* logs, plastered inside and out with clay mixed with dried grasses. Like most Creek families they had several houses—a summer house a short distance away from the winter house, and two storehouses. The summer house was also built of logs, but the gable ends were open to catch the breezes. One of the storehouses was for furs and the other for storing vegetables and other foods.

The Southeastern Indians enjoyed a food supply that included both wild and domesticated foods, with wild foods the more basic source. Some of their hunting, fishing, and gathering techniques were more than 9,000 years old. With simple technology, their hunting strategy was not so much concerned with hitting the animal from a distance as getting so close to the animal that they could not miss. In the latter part of the seventeenth century, before British traders made the gun generally available to them, the Indians' main weapon was the bow and arrow. Their main game animal, the white-tailed deer, provided almost 90 percent of the animal protein in their diet.

No decent warrior hunted without praying for the forgiveness of the animal to be hunted.

> *Give me the wind. Give me the breeze. Yu!*
> *Let my good dreams develop; let my little*
> *trails be directed, as they lie in various directions.*

This was directed to the two principal dieties of the hunter: Long Man the River, and Sacred Fire. And when the game was sighted, forgiveness was asked of the animal.

At the house, Tomo-chi-chi greeted his mother who was grinding corn with a heavy mortar. His grandmother sat by the open door, working at a small loom. The smoke from her tiny clay pipe was sweet. It was Creek custom that relatives of the mother live together. The household or *huti* might also include aged or dependent members of the mother's clan. Tomo-chi-chi ate a hearty breakfast of *softee*, fish and pumpkin bread, then talked about what he would be doing at the *puskita*. On the eve of October, "big chestnut month," he could see nothing but good happening.

He looked forward to watching as the sacred fires were rekindled, and to the ceremony of the sacred drink. In their own language, the Creeks called the brew "white drink" because white symbolized purity, happiness, and social harmony. But the Europeans called it "black drink" because of its color. Made from the leaves of a variety of holly its main ingredient was caffeine. Tomo-chi-chi was not yet old enough to join in this ceremony. Only the grown men, never the young or women, were allowed to consume the drink of purification.

Still, he was excited about talking with the Second Men who would be preparing the black drink, and with the Great Warrior (*tastanagi tako*) who was in charge of the ball games. The Great Warrior was the war chief who carried out the will of the *mico*. These men all sat in the Creek council at the town house. There were also the "Beloved Old Men (*isti atcagagi*)", men who had distinguished themselves in many ways and were considered the wise men, of *puskita*.

"Some day," Tomo-chi-chi told his mother, "I will be a wise man. I will be *mico* and in my old age, a Beloved Old Man. She looked at him lovingly. He was a dreamer, this son, and she hoped that his dreams would come true.

*The English hold on the Indians had been much
shaken by the frightful Yamassee War, but
it had not been completely broken, and the
Carolinians after 1716 set resolutely to work
to win back the friendship of the Creeks.*

—John Pitts Corry

Chapter Two

THE CREEKS HAD A STRONG SENSE OF UNITY
even though the Nation was made up of many tribes. In addition to the many tribal languages, one language was spoken that was understood by all the tribes. *Muskogean* was the most important language family in the Southeast. But until the mid-nineteenth century, there was no alphabet, no written language among the Creeks or any Indians. Legends and stories passed down through generations were the way that history was taught. Indian children grew up to become eloquent speakers. They spoke with a poetry that reflected the life around them: the silvery fall of mountain rain, the wind keening through ancient trees, the graceful flight of deer, the majesty of black wolves that cried in the night. Their language sounded of the earth and was beautiful.

Tomo-chi-chi grew up to be an eloquent spokesman for his people. Even as a young man, he was respected for his good judgment and wisdom. He was often consulted in matters of politics and law.

Very little is known about Tomo-chi-chi's life as a young

and middle-aged man. Because there was no written language among the Creeks, there were no records, no diaries, no letters until the arrival of the various colonists. Tomo-chi-chi evidently remained at Coweta during this period of his life. A few years after he became a warrior, he married a young woman named Senawki, with whom he'd grown up in the village. He built her a cabin of *wisso* and furnished it with deerskins. His young wife cleaned the furs and softened them for the couches and beds. She made beautiful pottery, which she decorated with bright paints. In their summer house, she spread the floor with sweet-smelling herbs of pennyroyal and mint to guard against mosquitoes and fleas.

As a young warrior, Tomo-chi-chi hunted in the forests and fields. Once, on a hunting party with his friend Chigelley, they stopped to rest. They had ridden into a wide, lush valley surrounded by distant hills when a sound like thunder caused them to rein in their horses. In the distance, a low cloud moved across the horizon.

Buffalo moved across the fields, leaving a red cloud of dust in their wake. As the huge animals moved closer, their massive bodies seemed resigned and patient, as though they moved in blindness.

"There are not as many of them as there were," said Tomo-chi-chi, gazing out at the herd.

"No," said Chigelley. "They have been killed in great numbers by the whites. Our people take them for food and hides, but there are some whites who kill them for their tongues, leaving the animals to die and rot."

Chigelly looked over at his friend. Tomo-chi-chi was a few years older than he, and was tall and well built. He was a full-blood and wore the mark of his Creek ancestors proudly. His nose was aquiline, his cheekbones high and sharp, his eyes so dark that the irises seemed invisible.

They rode on and shortly before reaching the village, came to a field covered with goldenrod. Suddenly the sky darkened. The air filled with the whirring of wings as passenger pigeons, thousands and thousands of them, flew across the sky. The bright morning darkened as the birds flew, blotting out the sun.

"*Wa-ah*," said Tomo-chi-chi, pointing to the birds. "The pigeons fly away from this place."

"It's an omen," said Chigelley, darkly. "It means the whites are coming, taking over our places." He was not fond of whites. He didn't trust them. In time, when he became Second Man to Old Brim, he and his friend, Tomo-chi-chi would have harsh words about this issue.

As they hunted for food, the young men of the villages would be gone for weeks at a time, traveling the narrow paths of the forests. Because these paths were so narrow, they were traveled single-file, Indian fashion. The trails were marked in secret ways, unknown to any but the Indian. There might be a tiny pile of stones, a mark on a tree just barely visible to one who knew how to search, or a stick figure carved on a tree trunk or a rock and hidden by moss and leaves. These signs were road maps to those who could read them.

These paths were also used by Indian traders who traveled from tribe to tribe throughout the territory. The traders spoke a language called *Mobilian*, a combination of all the tribal languages with words that were understood by all. Moving from place to place, the traders exchanged shells from the coastal Indians for the clay pipes of the Upper Creeks. Saddles fashioned by the Cherokees were much prized and could be traded for pearls or gunpowder. Flints were traded for salt, furs for various goods from copper pans to silk petticoats.

With more and more traders coming into Indian territory, the face of Indian life changed. In 1673, when Tomo-chi-chi was twenty-three, French explorers Jacques Marquette and Louis Joliet reached the headwaters of the Mississippi River. The fur trade, especially in deerskins, was becoming more and more valuable to the three world powers. Britain, France, and Spain were gradually encroaching on the territory of the Southeastern Indians, colonizing their land and using them to further their own ends, and each worked to defeat their enemies. It was Britain's relations with the Southeastern Indian that changed and colored Tomo-chi-chi's life and those of his people.

More and more traders entered Indian territory. Guns and ammunitions were easier to obtain and made war easier to wage. Hunting became a business rather than a means for eating and survival. Tribal wars over hunting territories began and the Indian world became more violent. Rivalry between the white traders divided the Indian tribes as the British, French, and Spanish each courted the Indians for their trade and loyalty. Indian lands were fair game, and were simply taken over and occupied by Europeans.

For centuries, a chain of islands off the Georgia coast were unknown except to the early Creek inhabitants of the coastal plains of the Atlantic. Then, in 1540, the islands were seized by Spanish conquistadors as outposts of Spain. When King Charles extended the English claim in 1665 as far south as St. Augustine, the islands were given the names by which they have been historically known ever since: *Ossabaw, Sapelo,* and St. Catherine's. The English coming to Carolina in 1670 had found the Spaniards in possession of the coast from St. Augustine northward to St. Catherine's Island. Step by step, the newcomers began to press the Spaniards back to the southern frontier. And in 1680, aided by Yamassee Indians whom they had won to their support, the Carolinians attacked the mission on St. Catherine's Island. While the Carolinians were turned back, the Indians at the mission left and fled southward, followed by the Spaniards. The Spaniards then withdrew to Sapelo Island.

The next step in the English offensive was taken by the Scots who had founded a colony at Port Royal in the

Carolinas. The Spaniards retaliated and wiped out the colony. Nevertheless, the Spanish Governor Cabrera thought it prudent to withdraw to Amelia Island. While English pressure was being exerted along the coast, Spanish missions along the Chattahoochee River were being threatened by the coming of Carolina traders. Most of the Creeks who lived near the missions declared their loyalty to the English. Up until then, the area had been peaceful for both the Creek Indians and the Carolinians. There were a few minor skirmishes, but for the most part life was serene and pleasant. The Creeks fought occasional battles with their long-standing enemies, the Cherokees, but that was minor. Now the Creeks were being courted by new-comers to the land: the Spanish and English and French settlers who needed their support in fighting one another.

Then something unexpected happened. In 1714, the Yamassee Indians, who had long patrolled the borders between the Carolinas and the southernmost territories, struck suddenly and hard at the Carolina settlements. Sick of being cheated by the traders, of having their people persecuted and taken into slavery by the whites for the British West Indies plantations, the Yamassee began a small rebellion. Traders reported hostilities in villages along the trade routes. The Yamassee War began in earnest in 1715 when Thomas Nairne, the Indian agent for South Carolina, was killed by Yamassees.

By the end of 1716, an uneasy peace had been restored but the English hold on the Creeks had been shaken. Old Brim, the chief *mico* of the Upper and Lower Creek Nation, held a meeting in Coweta. Tomo-chi-chi sat with him as counsel as did his friend, Chigelley. Old Brim was inclined to support the English cause, as was Tomo-chi-chi. The Carolinians set out to please the Creek *mico* by agreeing to stop the unfair and unkind trading practices that had occurred in the past.

Governor Middleton of South Carolina sent an emmissary to Coweta. Tobias Fitch made several journeys between Charles Town and the Creek towns, making every effort to win back the support of the Creeks. Eventually, the talks worked and the Creeks agreed to support the English cause. The Yamassees, on the other hand, supported the Spanish cause. In time, the government of South Carolina passed laws that made it necessary for traders to register and obtain licenses before selling goods to the Indians. But many of the traders ignored the laws and continued to do as they pleased, cheating on weights and measures and selling shoddy goods.

In 1717, the British were considering setting up a buffer colony for Carolina in the low country, intending to occupy the land between the Savannah and the Altamaha Rivers, the exact region which later became Georgia. These plans were later abandoned but the British government realized that it was necessary to protect their southern colonies and stated their intention of so doing.

The (Creek) towns sometimes split, sometimes amicably
and sometimes not, with one faction moving away
to establish a new town. Initially the town continued
to be a part of the chiefdom, or tal'wa, but in time
it might acquire a social identity of its own.

—Charles Hudson

Chapter Three

MISTS ROSE FROM THE RIVER, CLOAKING THE
village of Coweta and hiding all but the tops of the trees.
A soft peeping of birdsong had begun, and wisps of smoke
rose from the chimneys of the houses and from the summer
lodge. People were gathering in the square, some on horseback, some on foot. Some were leaving, others were bidding them farewell.

In the summer of 1725, when he was nearly seventy-five
years old, Tomo-chi-chi, his wife Senawki, and their young,
adopted son, Tooanahowie, left their village for the low
country. This could not have been an easy decision for
Tomo-chi-chi. He was an old man, although he didn't look
it. Paintings of him show a man who looks twenty-five
years younger than his actual age.

There are no records to show why he left. Historians,
writing about him as seen through the eyes of white
colonists, report that he had been "banished" by his people. Yet, more than 100 other Creeks—men, women, and
children—left with him. Historians state that it was not

14

because of any ill will, or that it was punishment for a specific crime or general misconduct. More likely, it was because of political disagreements. Given the times, and the way many of the Creeks viewed the British colonists who were settling the area, there may have been harsh feelings between those Indians who welcomed the whites and those who resented them.

Now, he was bidding farewell to the life he had known, and was starting over again. A crowd gathered around him. Standing next to him, Senawki held Tooanahowie. He was only a year-old but was almost too big for his carrier. The child was Tomo-chi-chi's great nephew whom he had adopted after the death of the boy's parents. Creeks enjoyed extended families, often including among their households aging parents, relatives, orphans, and even individuals who had been captured in war and adopted into the clan. Also standing nearby were several men and their families who would follow Tomo-chi-chi to the "old fields." Among them were Hillispilli, who would serve as Second Man to Tomo-chi-chi, and Stimaulki, brother of Senawki.

In this late summer, Tomo-chi-chi wore traditional Creek dress of leggings of soft deerskin for travel through the forest, and moccasins that were cut from a single piece of deerskin, with one seam up the back of the foot and another on top of the foot. These were worn only when they were traveling or when the weather was cold. His chest was bare and a deerskin was draped over one shoulder. Senawki wore a loose blouse fashioned of doeskin and embroidered in tiny, blue beads in a pattern of flowers. Her skirt was made of a kind of cloth woven from the inner bark of the mulberry tree. Tall and slender, she carried Tooanahowie lightly on her back in his carrier. Tomo-chi-chi turned to go. He moved easily through the crowd, walking lightly on the balls of his feet, his back straight.

There was something mystical about his move to the coast. It was as though he heard other voices, other sounds

15

calling him back to the place of his ancestors. The site chosen for the new village was one that was familiar to the Creeks. It was the site of the "old fields," the place of the sacred mounds where many of their ancestors were buried. It was also close to the sacred "hunting islands" of *Sapelo, Ossabaw,* and St. Catherine's that the Creeks had declared as their own. These islands off the coast were visited by Creeks from all over the Nation. There, they hunted and fished and harvested the huge oyster beds.

There was no turning back now for Tomo-chi-chi. He had held the carved bowl of the sacred pipe with reverent fingers. He had smoked the pipe of peace. He had prayed to the Grandfathers, smoking the sacred tobacco and sending the smoke into the four directions of the earth: north, south, east, and west. He had chosen the path and now walked it.

It took courage to leave the known for the unknown. In 1725, the area around Savannah Town was dangerous. For nearly thirty-five years, the place had been the focus of all the trails to the west. The Spanish had long coveted the lands around the coast and the French and Spanish-allied Yamassee Indians were not far away in Florida.

And so, Tomo-chi-chi returned to the place of his ancestors. He now wore an eagle's feather twisted in his braid to show his rank of *mico*. The rank was new for him. Up until now, he had been considered one of the Beloved Men, an elder respected and whose counsel was sought. Like the holy men, the priests, Tomo-chi-chi could read the bones and hear the dead speak. And for him, there were reasons beyond politics to return to the old fields. It was there that the spirits of the dead were and where the voices of the ancestors could still be heard. Indians are never far from their dead. Tomo-chi-chi had walked on the earth for many winters. He had listened to the voice of Long Man the River and had read the future in the green mosses of the rocks. There was a good reason to return to the sacred old fields. In time, the reason would be revealed to him.

The village of Yamacraw was built on the steep bluffs high above the Savannah River. It was the only settlement between the Carolina border and the wilderness beyond. It was laid out in the traditional way. The houses were built with a rectangular floor plan and gabled roofs. Oystershell paths linked the village to the bluffs. Around the plaza were the council house, the town house, and a *chungke* field. Yamacraw was shaded by ancient, live oaks and magnolias. Below, the river formed a half-moon where it flowed into the sea. At the mouth of the river lay an island called Tybee. There, herons and cranes moved on stilt-like legs, searching for food in the salt marshes. Right whales swam in the clear green waters off the coast on their way to warmer seas to bear their young.

Soon after the village was settled, Tomo-chi-chi received word that Old Brim had died. Chigelley would serve as *mico* until Malatchi, Old Brim's son, was of age. Chigelley suggested that a trading post be opened where the Indians could trade goods with the English whenever they wished, rather than depending on the traders to come to them. It was also suggested that it would be good if the person running the post were Indian or, if not, at least someone with an understanding of the Creeks. The person chosen was both of these.

Mary Musgrove, whose Creek name was *Coosaponakeesa*, had grown up at Coweta. Her mother, who was the sister of Old Brim, had married an English trader from Carolina. Mary had been raised partly in Coweta among the Creeks, and partly in South Carolina among her father's people. She and Malatchi, the son of Old Brim, had grown up together and were best friends and cousins. Towards the end of the border wars, she met young John Musgrove, whose father, Captain Musgrove, was instrumental in working out the treaty establishing the new border between the Creeks and the Carolinians. Mary and

John Musgrove were married and moved to Charles Town. Their marriage had been a political one.

When Tomo-chi-chi learned that Mary would be coming from Charles Town with her husband, John, to build and open the trading post in Indian territory, he was delighted. He had known Mary, or *Coosaponakeesa*, as a child. She had left Coweta with her new husband before Tomo-chi-chi left Coweta, but he remembered her. She had been a pretty child, small, with dark hair and grey eyes.

"She's a woman now," said Senawki, who had seen the young girl grow up. "I'm glad she'll be here with us. She belongs here, not in that place where she lives only with the whites."

Tomo-chi-chi offered the use of land along the wide and gentle Altamaha River for the trading post. It was a good site, high and accessible by both the western trail and the old trading path leading from the Western boundary of the Lower Creek Nation. The post would be situated north of the village, near the sacred old fields.

In April, 1730, Mary and John Musgrove left Charles Town for Port Royal. From there they would be taken across the river to the village of Yamacraw where they would stay with "her people" until a house could be built for them.

At Port Royal, sailors helped with their luggage, stowing it away on board a piragua. Much larger than a canoe, the piragua was made of a hollowed out cypress or cedar log. It had a square stern with a cabin, and another smaller deck was built in the sharp bow. Mary got her first glimpse of Tybee Island on an early May morning. Sands gleamed brilliant white. The oaks of the island were stunted, blown by the winds into odd shapes. At the northern tip of the island, dolphins rode the bow waves of the boat, their silvery bodies shining in the green waters. Mary tasted the salt spray on her lips and smelled the clean iodine scent of marsh. She was happy to be leaving

18

Charles Town and she was looking forward to seeing her kinsman, Tomo-chi-chi, again.

Tomo-chi-chi waited on shore as the piragua docked at the foot of Pipemaker's Bluff. Senawki and Tooanahowie waited with him. Below them, the river was clear and green. Giant turtles floated in the cool water like strange, moving rocks. Birdsong and the sweet scent of wild orange blossoms drifted out over the water. Suddenly, Tooana-howie could stand the suspense no longer. He raced down the bluff and out to the water's edge. He called out a greeting to Mary. Delighted, she asked his name.

"Tooanahowie," he shouted back, his face bright with laughter, his dark hair shining in the sun. "My name is Tooanahowie and I'm going to be *mico* one day!" He was six years old.

Tomo-chi-chi assigned braves to help with building and stocking the trading post, which would be called Mount Venture. In return for their services, the Creeks paid the Musgroves 1,500 pounds of furs annually, and the Carolina government paid them in gold. While John was overseeing the construction of the post, Mary was overseeing the building of a house in what would later become the town of Savannah.

Tomo-chi-chi and Mary were of the Wind Clan, and "from the same fire." The old *mico* welcomed her and gave her an outright gift of land: a tract of some 500 acres on which to build a house and cow pens. Tomo-chi-chi made it clear that these lands were Mary's for her own use. Although Indians did not accept the idea of individuals owning the land, Chigelley and Tomo-chi-chi "gave" land to Mary. Perhaps they were aware that among the English land was a thing to be kept, a kind of insurance. At that time, Indian women owned their houses, English women did not. But because Mary was considered Creek and of his clan, Tomo-chi-chi protected her and her rights.

By early December, the trading post was stocked with

supplies and provided a place for a mail drop. John spent most of his time there while Mary worked at the house in town, planting a fall garden and stocking the cow pens with cattle ordered from South Carolina. Trade had increased along the trails from the mountains and from the Carolinas. And Mary and Tomo-chi-chi both stayed aware of any new developments.

I had a dream about the cranes. In my
dream, they flew twice.

—Tomo-chi-chi

Chapter Four

ON A MILD, SUNNY DAY IN LATE DECEMBER,
1732, Tomo-chi-chi, Mary, and Tooanahowie walked down
the beach at St. Catherine's Island. They had come over
with others to forage oysters from the giant reef just offshore.
Earlier, Tooanahowie had been spear-fishing for the flounders that lay in the shallows at the edge of the surf. At eight
years, he was tall for his age, strong, and capable. The breeze
was out of the south, and above them, the blue sky held
clusters of clouds low on the horizon. Tooanahowie and
Mary had a surprise for Tomo-chi-chi, and after their meal,
they would give the old *mico* something he'd always wanted.

In the distance, a group of girls searched the woods for
the *smilax* vine that grew thickly in the tops of the live
oaks. The roots were edible and best when gathered in
early winter. They would also be digging out the "swamp
potatoes," which were the root of the arrowhead plant.
Excursions to the islands always produced a variety of the
plants and berries loved by the Indians. Mary had picked a
basket of scuppernongs, wild grapes with thick, bronze
skins whose fragrance permeated the woods. Young boys
climbed the persimmon trees for the ripe, pulpy fruit that
tasted date-like and cool.

When the others grew busy with the afternoon meal, the three of them slipped away. Tooanahowie built a fire, using four sticks to hold up the grill he'd made of green branches on which to cook the fish. They cooked corn in the husk and ate the sweet scuppernongs and persimmons. Creeks preferred their fruits and berries raw, but ate very few raw vegetables. Vegetables were cooked, made into stews, or ground for various breads.

After the meal, they sat on the sands in the shadows of the stunted oaks, looking out at sea. The breeze smelled of cedar and salt marsh. Tooanahowie added driftwood to the fire. It was time to give Tomo-chi-chi his "surprise." It had long been Tomo-chi-chi's dream that "his" children learn to read the "talking leaves," as he called books. For months, Mary had been teaching Tooanahowie to read and write. Now, picking up a stick, she began writing letters in the damp sands. There was no Creek alphabet, so she had taught Tooanahowie to read in English. She drew a *T* in the sands, then wrote Tomo-chi-chi's name. Then she wrote a sentence from *The Book of Common Prayer*, from which she'd been teaching Tooanahowie:

> O, ye Whales, and all that move in the waters,
> Bless ye the Lord: praise him, and magnify him forever.

When he heard his son read the words, the old *mico* was pleased. He wanted all the children to learn to read and write.

Feathers of rose brushed the edges of the sky. At sunset, hundreds of silver dolphins split the water into curves of gold as they came into the sound to feed. Tomo-chi-chi, Tooanahowie, and Mary watched until the dolphins swam farther out to sea and disappeared.

Then, a crane's call rang clear and low over the water. "Garooo-a-a-a" was repeated again and again. Sandhill cranes, ponderously beautiful, circled the beach and began slowing their flight. Their plumage of pale ash and blue mingled with the colors of evening as their great wings beat on the air. One by one they dropped on long, slender legs into the sea. When the last of them had landed and floated lightly on the water, Tomo-chi-chi said, "I had a dream about the cranes. In my dream, they flew twice. Once to tell me of a man who is to come, and once to tell me of a man who is no more on this earth. The first man comes soon, I think."

Mary never doubted Tomo-chi-chi's words or his visions. He had dreams and saw things. He knew the ways of wild things and how to read the messages they sent. Tomo-chi-chi was a wise man.

Seagrass made a rattling sound in the sea breeze. The fire burned blue, coral, and green from the driftwood. In the deepening twilight, the scattering of campfires on the beach were pinpricks against the coming night. The phosphorescence in the sea glowed like a wash of green stars, reflecting the heavens. Shooting stars arched across the heavens and seemed to fall into the sea.

*Tomo-chi-chi was a Creek Indian, and in his youth
a great warrior. He had an excellent judgment and
a very ready wit, which showed itself in his answers
on all occasions.*

—James Edward Oglethorpe

Chapter Five

IN THE PRE-DAWN OF A MILD, JANUARY DAY IN 1733, Tomo-chi-chi walked back from the burial mound where his ancestors lay. He had listened to the voices and knew that today, the man he had seen in his dreams would arrive. The narrow path leading back to the bluff was shaded by ancient trees hung with soft, grey moss. Draping the low branches, yellow jasmine was not yet open to the day's warmth when it would scent the air with sweetness. A sea-gull flew low overhead, its wings black against the rising sun. *The man would come this day,* Tomo-chi-chi thought. He had only a feeling of anticipation and no thought of dread.

Later that same morning Mary was at her cabin, dragging feather ticks out into the sun. As she laid them out to freshen on pine boughs, she heard a slight sound behind her. Tooanahowie stood there, his face bright with anticipation. "Tomo-chi-chi says to come with me! Somebody's coming! He needs you to talk!"

She glanced down at her red petticoat which she'd pulled on over her shift. "Come now!" said Tooanahowie, taking her by the hand. "You have to talk!"

Mary acted as interpreter for Tomo-chi-chi in any dealings with the English. She spoke English, *Mobilian* and *Muskogean*, and he trusted her implicitly. "Yes, my young lord," she laughed, following him down the path that led to the bluffs. "Lead the way."

From the woods came the sound of people moving, a faint rustling like leaves blown by the wind. The villagers were going to the bluffs to greet the visitors who were approaching by sea.

Tomo-chi-chi stood on the high bluff overlooking the shining river. Behind him, the ancient forest was shadowy and deep. A slight breeze ruffled the surface of the water and stirred the feathers of his matchcoat, which was fashioned from the feathers of a hundred birds. Next to him were Mary, Senawki, and Tooanahowie.

On both sides of the river the land rose into high cliffs crowned with ancient trees. Birdsong was sweet, the clear notes sounding in ripples and trills. The mingled scent of flowers and leaves was blown out to the river where the reflection of the land shimmered in a mirrored image. Leaving only a small wake in the green water, the piragua approached the foot of the bluffs. On board were James Edward Oglethorpe, newly arrived from England, and William Bull of South Carolina. While the crew of four sailors prepared to dock, Oglethorpe prepared to disembark. Tomo-chi-chi watched as the tall, handsome Englishman began walking up the steep bluff. "This is the man," he said softly to Mary, "this is the man I saw in my dream."

James Edward Oglethorpe was forty-four years old when he began his new venture in bringing unfortunate debtors and the deserving poor to the new world. His Army career had ended in England with the beginning of peace in 1718. He had returned to his family estate in Godalming and there entered politics. In 1722 he was elected to Parliament. Instrumental in the passage of the Debtor's Act in 1730, which for the first time allowed British debtors some rights under law, Oglethorpe extended his concern for the poor and debt–ridden of England. Together with a group of men equally concerned, they drew up a plan to create a haven for the poor and oppressed, and for any honest men and women who wanted to start a new life in a new land.

Oglethorpe had arrived at Charles Town from Gravesend, England, on January 16, 1733 on board *The Anne*, leaving Captain Thomas and 130 passengers at safe harbor, After meeting with Governor Robert Johnson of South Carolina, Oglethorpe left for Port Royal, and then to Savannah with William Bull. Establishing a haven for the poor was an admirable undertaking, but in truth Oglethorpe was offered help from the Carolinians for other reasons. A buffer was needed as a protection, especially for Carolina, against Spain. The British government realized that it needed to protect their Southern colonies, and when Oglethorpe's philanthropic plan was laid before it, it was readily accepted. Brought about by political necessity, but for Oglethorpe, born of the highest principles, the Colony of Georgia was established.

Just before he reached the top of the bluff, a flutter of red caught Oglethorpe's eye. Then he saw the small band of Indians waiting for him. Next to the small woman in the red petticoat, stood a tall, handsome warrior in a match-coat of blue and brown feathers that melded into the colors of the forest. The old man wore an eagle's feather in his hair. Standing beside him and the woman was a young boy. These, then, were the Yamacraws about whom he'd been told in Charles Town. As Oglethorpe walked from dense shade into sunlight, his wig gleamed silver and the buttons on his deep blue coat burned and glittered. Smiling at the assembled group, Oglethorpe made a deep bow and extended his hand in greeting.

"On behalf of His Royal Majesty, King George II, I extend greetings," he said, wondering as he did if anyone there could understand one word he said.

26

Mary Musgrove stepped forward as Tomo-chi-chi's interpreter. She curtsied, then welcomed him to Savannah Town on behalf of the Yamacraws. On board the piragua, William Bull waited for a signal from Oglethorpe. At the sign, Bull joined him, and when the introductions were complete, they were invited by Tomo-chi-chi to visit the lodge house and smoke the pipe of peace.

The lodge house was smoky and warm, the air pungent with the scent of burning herbs, pine, furs, and tobacco. When the pipe had been smoked and passed around, two warriors entered the room. They carried conch shells filled with the sacred black drink. Tomo-chi-chi and his Second Man, Hillispilli, drank first. Then the shells were passed to the others especially chosen. Nearby, the Beloved Women sat watching, Senawki among them. Mary sat with the men, her role as interpreter allowing her an honored place.

Oglethorpe explained his mission. He told of his plans for a new colony and what it would mean in terms of freedom and peace for the settlers. Tomo-chi-chi then explained that permission would have to be obtained from Chigelley, and *micos* of other tribes within the Nation. In the meantime, however, Tomo-chi-chi offered his protection to the settlers whenever they came. And he made a request. "In return for our protection, I would have our children taught to read the 'talking leaves.'"

When Oglethorpe agreed, Tomo-chi-chi told him that the other chiefs would be notified, and that a meeting would be held at Yamacraw to discuss the terms of the agreement between them. When the meeting ended, Mary Musgrove had been offered a job as interpreter for Oglethorpe. She would receive a salary of 200 pounds sterling a year.

And from these talks Tomo-chi-chi, the man of peace from one of the "white" towns of peace, and the man from England with a message of peace, began a friendship that was to last their lifetimes. Tomo-chi-chi, whose *tal'wa* was peace, offered new life to the settlers. The talks, which

27

began in a rough lodge in an ancient forest, would continue in palaces in England. Tomo-chi-chi, the warrior with words, would speak with kings and queens, bishops and archbishops, professors and students, in his role as spokesman and diplomat for his people.

But could this man, old before the nation was young, bring about a peaceful establishment of a new colony in a new land? His message went out to the other chiefs. Tomo-chi-chi himself had welcomed the English. His eloquence would need to be enough to convince his people to do the same.

There are in Georgia, on this side of the mountains,
three considerable nations of Indians; one called
the Lower Creeks, consisting of nine towns, making
about a thousand men able to bear arms.

—James Edward Oglethorpe

Chapter Six

OGLETHORPE RETURNED TO CHARLES TOWN
to escort *The Anne* and her passengers to Savannah. In a
letter to the Trustees written just after his meeting with
Tomo-chi-chi, Oglethorpe wrote:

> ...The whole people arrived here on the first of February.
> At night their tents were set up...A little Indian nation,
> the only one within fifty miles, is not only at Amity, but
> desirous to be Subjects to His Majesty King George, to
> have lands given them among us, and to educate their chil-
> dren at our schools. . .

The Indians welcomed the new settlers with gifts of
goods—fresh venison, fish and bread, fruits and root vegetables. On the morning after their arrival, Oglethorpe met
with his people to thank God for safe conduct and to ask
His blessing upon the new settlement. "It is my hope," said
Oglethorpe, "that through your good example the settlement of Georgia may prove a blessing and not a curse to
the native inhabitants."

After supplies were issued to them, the settlers were assigned tasks. Oglethorpe explained the necessity for laboring in common until the site for the town was cleared and housing built. Some of the men were detailed to work on the construction of a crane on the docks for unloading supplies that would be coming from England. Others began felling the tall pines on the bluff, and with the help of braves from the Yamacraw village, began building shelters of logs, roofed with palmetto fronds to keep out the rain. By nightfall of the first day, the women and children were sleeping in shelters.

The rains began a few days later, but they were soft and gentle and did nothing to dampen the spirits of the new settlers. Georgia's climate in February was still much warmer and more pleasant than England's. The Carolinians, in an effort to help the new settlement, sent sawyers and carpenters to Savannah. Houses were built and a few public buildings. The smell of sawdust and woodsmoke drifted over the settlement.

In March, raw winds from the sea howled and blew around the tiny houses, chilling the occupants and sending smoke billowing into the small rooms. Later in the month, when the ground had warmed, fields were cleared and the Indians volunteered to help with spring planting. They showed the settlers how to plant Indian corn together with beans and squash. The "three sisters" were soon growing in every settler's garden.

During the month of March, 1733, colonists continued to arrive in Savannah from London by way of Charles Town. The first wheat crop had been planted by Mary Musgrove. "The settlers will need bread," she told Tomo-chi-chi. The Indians also showed the settlers how to catch fish in maze-like traps made of bamboo and reeds, and to spear the flounders hidden in the soft sands of the beaches. Sharing the work with his people, Oglethorpe was busy encouraging and supervising.

Soon, the general outline of Savannah could be seen. So

far, of course, only the Yamacraw had given their consent for the settlement, but the time of the meeting between Oglethorpe, Tomo-chi-chi, and the *micos* of the various tribes was set for May, 1733.

In late March, in a letter to the Trustees regarding the progress of the new colony, Oglethorpe wrote:

> The Savannah (river) has a very long course, and a great trade is carried on by the Indians, there having been twelve trading boats passed since I have been here. There are in Georgia, on this side of the mountains, three considerable nations of Indians; one called the Lower Creeks, consisting of nine towns, making about a thousand men able to bear arms. One of these is within a short distance of us and has concluded a peace with us, giving us the right of all this part of the Country. And I have marked out the lands which they have reserved for themselves. Their King (Tomo-chi-chi) comes constantly to Church, and has given me his nephew, a boy who is his next heir, to educate.

In May, Captain James Yoakley landed *The James* at Savannah with seventeen passengers who had been approved by the Trustees. Among them were Italians expert in working in the manufacture of raw silk. Because *The James* was the first ship from England to land directly at Savannah, without first docking at Charlestown, her captain was awarded a prize of money. According to *Gentleman's Magazine* in London:

> *Savannah, May 20th, 1733. The James*, Captain Yoakley, 110 tons and six guns, arrived here on the 14th with passengers and stores. The captain received the price appointed by the Trustees for the first ship that should unload at this Town, where is safe riding for much larger vessels.

Words are no return for kindness.
For good words may be spoken by the deceitful,
as well as by the upright heart.

—Tomo-chi-chi

Chapter Seven

THE MORNING DAWNED BRIGHT AND WARM. The *chungke* field was given a final smoothing by some of the young men, and a circle was cleared for dancing. Indian cradles swung from low branches, and young children tumbled and played on quilts laid in the shade of the live oaks. The scent of honeysuckle sweetened the air, and magnolia trees were starred with huge, lemony-sweet blossoms.

The various chiefs of the Creek tribes were meeting in Savannah to discuss the use of the land by the English. Fifty braves, representing nine tribes, began arriving. A meeting place had been chosen and the preparations begun. True to his promises, Tomo-chi-chi had exerted his influence on behalf of the colonists, and had sent messages to the various principal towns and chief men of the Creek tribes.

Great shanks of venison turned slowly on spits, the juices dripping onto the coals and sending up spurts of flame and fragrant smoke. Tables had been placed in the deep shade of live oak trees, and food prepared by both Creek women and women from the colony was set out for everyone.

The dress of the people gathered for the meeting was as

varied as the people themselves. Indians wore feathers and bright beads, some decorated their faces in scarlet and white paint, others wore the pale buff of deerskin. The women of the colony dressed according to their former status in England, Italy, or Germany. Young girls were dressed in light muslins, and their mothers wore more elaborate brocades and silks. Looking like starlings among peacocks, indentured servant girls moved among the tables wearing dull blues and browns.

Carolina Rangers, the lawmen for the territory, wore brightly checked shirts and coonskin caps. They were a tough group of men, hardened by living in the wilderness and patrolling the areas between the Carolina border and the new colony.

Tomo-chi-chi was the first *mico* to arrive. Although far advanced in years, his was a powerful presence. Still muscular, his back straight, he commanded attention as he walked through the crowd in his feathered matchcoat. His influence was great, yet he was modest and philosophical.

Chigelley had arrived from Coweta. As chief *mico* of the Upper and Lower Creek Nations, he took the place of honor next to Tomo-chi-chi and James Oglethorpe. With him was Malatchi, who would one day assume the role of chief *mico*. Although Tomo-chi-chi had offered the use of land to the English, without the consent and goodwill of Chigelley it would have been a difficult if not impossible alliance. Mary and John Musgrove sat nearby and served as interpreters. Small and petite in a dress of creamy white buckskin embroidered in flowers made of cowrie shells and tiny, blue beads, Mary seemed childlike in the midst of the men.

The Beloved Men sat together while Hillispilli sat on the opposite side of Tomo-chi-chi, along with several other Yamacraw braves. When the participants of the meeting were assembled, the customary exchange of gifts took place.

The chiefs and representatives of the colony were seated in the middle of the clearing. At a signal from the various chiefs, furs were brought to the head table by eight young braves, one from each of the eight towns. They laid the bundles of deerskins down in front of Oglethorpe. Then, the English, directed by Oglethorpe, distributed gifts for the Creeks.

> To each of the chiefs: *a laced coat, hat, and shirt.*
> To each of the warriors: *a gun and a mantle of duffle cloth.*

And to all of their attendants: *a barrel of gunpowder, four kegs of bullets, a piece of broadcloth, a piece of Irish linen, a cask of tobacco pipes, eight belts and cutlasses with gilt handles, tape and ink of all colors, and eight kegs of rum,* to be carried home to their towns.

When the gifts had been accepted and thanks exchanged, a young Creek brave moved through the crowd, entered the clearing, and sat in the shade of a tree. Kneeling, he began tapping lightly on a small drum, the sound as muted and soft as a heartbeat. Then another brave entered the clearing, wearing a cap of white swansdown and a breechclout. Around his legs hung strings of beads and shells that jingled as he moved. He carried a fan of swan's feathers decorated with tiny bells that chimed gently with each movement of the fan.

He began his dance slowly, his movements punctuated by the drum. Moving slowly around the center of the clearing, his feet in soft moccasins of deerskin made no sound at all. Only the sound of the bells and the beat of the drum disturbed the quiet. The setting sun gilded the feathers with gold and threw long shadows across the faces of the people. Going over to Oglethorpe, the brave touched his shoulders lightly with the feathers, a sign of peace and friendship.

Then Tomo-chi-chi spoke. "I came here to look for good lands near the tombs of my ancestors. Now, your trustees have sent your people here. At first, I feared you would drive us away. But you confirmed our land to us and instructed our children. We have already thanked you in the strongest words we could find, but words are no return for kindness. For good words may be spoken by the deceitful, as well as by the upright heart. The chief men of all our Nation are here to thank you for us; and before them I declare your goodness, and that here I design to die. For we love your people so well that with them we will live and die."

Then Chigelley spoke. "I have come all the way from Coweta. Twenty-five days' journey to see you. I came down that I might hear good things, for I knew that if I died on the way I should die in doing good, and what was said would be carried back to the Nation, and our children would reap the benefit of it. Our nation was once strong, and had ten towns; but we are now weak, and have but eight towns. You have comforted the vanquished, and have gathered them that were scattered like little birds before the eagle. We give leave to Tomo-chi-chi, Stimaulki, and Hillispilli, to call the kindred that love them out of each of the Creek towns, that they may come together and make one town."

Then, getting to his feet, James Oglethorpe spoke courteously. "I urge you to understand that in making this settlement, the English desire neither to dispossess nor to annoy your people. It is our earnest wish to live in peace and friendship with you all." He then explained the power of the British nation and the general object in founding the colony, and asked those assembled for a cession of the lands lying between the Savannah and Altamaha Rivers.

Thus, the treaty was signed. The English were granted the rights to the islands off the coast from Tybee to St. Simon's except for the sacred hunting islands of Ossabaw, Sapelo and St. Catherine's. And the use of all lands lying between the Savannah and Altamaha Rivers "from the ocean to the head of tide water, or as far up as the tide ebbs and flows."

Agreements were drawn up regarding the regulation of prices of goods, value of furs, and privileges of traders.

Hillispilli then spoke for the Indians, promising that the English

> which shall settle among us shall not be robbed or molested in their trade in our Nation. That if it shall so happen that any of our people should be mad, and either kill, beat, wound, or rob any of the English traders or their people, then we, the said Head Men of the towns aforesaid do engage to have justice done to the English, and for that purpose to deliver up any of our people who shall be guilty of the crimes aforesaid, to be tried by the English law, or by laws of our Nation, as the beloved man of the Trustees shall think fit.

The Indians then promised not to have any business with the Spanish or French and "to keep the talk in our hearts as long as the sun shall shine or the waters run in the rivers. We have each of us set down the mark of our families."

The pipe of peace was smoked and the treaty established. The treaty was then forwarded to the Trustees in London for their formal confirmation.

Several months later, a small group of Yamacraws paid a visit to Tomo-chi-chi. He received them in the lodge. Outside, a light rain drifted in from the sea. Smoke hung heavy on the air. After greeting the old *mico*, they told him they were unhappy with the new English who had arrived.

"They have taken over our lands," said one man. "We agreed to a friendship, but it has been abused."

"How?" asked Tomo-chi-chi, passing the pipe to the first man. "Have the English caused you trouble?"

"The English now believe they *own* the lands, the lands allowed for their *use*." Was this what the *mico* had in mind when he allowed them to settle?

To the Indians, land was sacred, to be cared for and respected, but not owned. Land was not for individual use, but for everyone to share. The earth was considered the mother of life, and some tribes refused to plow for fear of harming the earth-mother. They believed that spiritual forces joined human beings to all other living things. They were afraid that these forces would be disturbed by the settlers, because they plowed the earth with metal and felled trees in great numbers.

Tomo-chi-chi explained his reasons for allowing the English to settle near Yamacraw: they had something he wanted. It was something he'd wanted for his people ever since he had become aware of the value of reading and writing. He wanted books or "talking leaves" to open the mysteries to his people. He would allow the English to settle the lands, and in exchange, they would give his people the ability to read and write.

"I want our children to be educated," he said. "I will build a school where they will be taught." Words were the answer. Words made you strong without weapons. Until his people could read and write, they were at the mercy of the Spanish, French, and English. The white people wrote down laws and rules. Tomo-chi-chi wanted his people to be able to do the same.

If there were no words, he explained, there would be no story told of the Creeks and their time upon the earth. They and their deeds would pass away into dust, and only memories would remain. That was not enough.

Tomo-chi-chi had spoken.

An aged chief named Tomo-chi-chi, the mico or king
of Yamacraw, a man of an excellent understanding,
is so desirous of having the young people taught the
English language, that, notwithstanding his advanced
age, he has come over with me to obtain means.

—James Edward Oglethorpe

Chapter Eight

TOOANAHOWIE LED THE WAY INTO THE DEEP
woods where bay and magnolia trees grew in thick profu-
sion. With him were a party of young men, both Creek and
English. As they entered a grove of sweetgum trees, they
could hear the sharp, nasal cry of the black and red
birds . . . kent . . . kent . . . kent . . . The birds continued
their pecking as the young men passed beneath them on
their way to find the fledgling mulberry trees to take back
to town. They would provide the food for the silkworms
that were being housed in a new shed at the edge of the
public gardens. Thousands of trees would be planted both
in the public gardens and on the property of every new
landholder.

Each family was required to plant, within a given time,
100 mulberry trees on every ten acres cleared. Silk produc-
tion was to be Savannah's major industry and everyone was
to be involved in its manufacture. A way had been found to
preserve the eggs of the silkworms and 100,000 mulberry
trees would be planted. Tooanahowie was proud to be able to

38

help and to be a part of the work. And even though he was the youngest among the party, the others listened to him.

He enjoyed seeing the town progress. One by one, frame houses were built. To the east of the town, the public gardens had been laid out, one-half of it on the top of a hill overlooking the river. In the garden were tulip trees, magnolias, live oaks, pines, and sassafras that had been left standing as part of the ancient forest. The garden was laid out with crosswalks planted in orange trees and at the bottom of the garden, protected from the north winds, were exotic plants that had been brought by ship from far-off places. Coffee had been planted, along with bamboo, figs, peaches, and curious herbs.

On the banks above the river, the town hall was under construction. A site had been chosen for the church and a small plot of ground for a cemetery. Plans were drawn for the building of a lighthouse at Tybee to guide ships entering the Savannah River.

In July, at a public meeting, Oglethorpe announced the plan of the town, how it was to be laid out and the names of the squares and the streets. He planned a series of squares— open spaces for trees and flowers—that would be built throughout the town. The first, called Johnson Square, was the model for the others to follow, and was named for Robert Johnson, the governor of South Carolina.

Savannah was becoming a haven for the persecuted and a place of hope for the poor. In January, 1734, under the conduct of Baron Philip Von Reck, a party of 78 Salzburgers arrived in Georgia from Austria. From 1729 to 1732, more than 30,000 Salzburgers left their homes in Germany to seek refuge from religious persecution in Prussia, Holland, and England. In London, they were offered asylum in Georgia. They were welcomed at Charles Town by Oglethorpe, who chanced to be there on business,

In his journal, the baron wrote that "Mr. Oglethorpe sent on board a large quantity of beef, two butts of wine, two tunn of *spring water, cabbage, turnips, radishes, and fruits, as a present from the Trustees."*

Three days later on Reminiscere Sunday in the Lutheran calendar, the Salzburgers docked at Savannah. They later settled the town of Springfield, in Effingham County, not far from Savannah. Baron Von Reck made a note in his journal that *"The earth is so fertile that it will bring forth anything that can be sown or planted in it."* After visiting Savannah, he described it as a *"happy place where plenty and brotherly love seem to make their abode, and where the good order of a nightly watch restrains the disorderly."*

Shortly after the first of the year, Oglethorpe planned a trip to England. He asked Tomo-chi-chi to go with him. Never having been out of his own land, Tomo-chi-chi asked many questions about where he would go, and what he would see. He was eighty-four years old and yet never hesitated for a moment to accept the new challenge. Senawki, her brother Stimaulki, Hillispilli, Tooanahowie, and four other Creek braves would accompany him. Mary Musgrove was asked to go as interpreter.

As soon as he learned he was to go to England, Tooanahowie was so excited he could hardly stand it. He'd never been on a big ship except when he investigated one that was tied up at the dock. The farthest he'd ever been was Coweta. But he was ready. He'd been practicing his English and could now recite the Lord's Prayer. He could also read from the *Book of Common Prayer*, and knew several prayers by heart. He was on very good terms with both the spirits of the Grandfathers and of the English God, and prayed to all of them.

The more he thought about what a wonderful place the world was, the more excited he became. He was going to take a voyage on a ship across the sea! Shortly before he was due to leave, he went to talk to his kinswoman, Mary Musgrove. At her plantation, he walked past the cowpens and stopped to admire the newest calves.

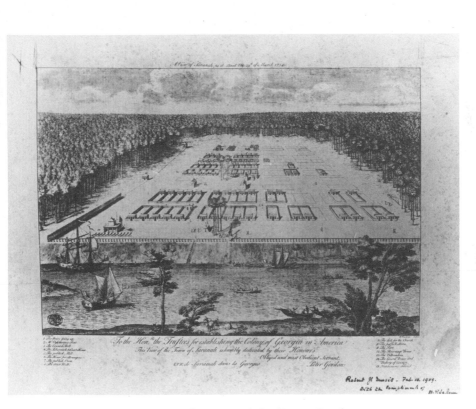

1734 view of Savannah by Peter Gordon.

It was a sunny, March morning. The earth smelled rich and good. The scent of pine smoke drifted on the air and mingled with the sweet fragrance of yellow jasmine. A cow scratched her rump against the fence. Suddenly, Tooana-howie just had to shout! Whooping and yelling, he went from gate to gate, opening them and shooing the cows out into the yard.

Mary was working in the stillroom, mixing a potion of fresh herbs when she heard the noise outside. Throwing open the shutters, she saw what Tooanahowie had done. Sending her overseer out to help round up the cattle, she then went to the storeroom for a shovel. Handing it to Tooanahowie, she sent him into the barn to get rid of more than his excitement.

A short time later, a runner appeared at the house with a message from Malatchi. Mary's parents were gravely ill at Coweta. She packed and prepared to go to them. In her absence, her husband, John, agreed to go to England in her place.

On the 7th of April, 1734, the *Aldborough* sailed from Charlestown for England. Since there was only the group from Savannah on board as passengers, Tooanahowie had the run of the ship. And he made the most of it. The sailors taught him how to navigate by the stars and to climb the rigging. While Senawki watched anxiously from the deck, Tooanahowie climbed the rigging almost to the crow's nest.

He watched friendly dolphins plowing the waves along the ship's bow, always running ahead. The sailors told him that dolphins were good luck for ships and sailors. One evening, there was a cry from the crow's nest.

"There she blows! Off the starboard bow!"

Everyone ran to the side of the ship, amazed to see twin spouts appear on the horizon. Right whales, black as night, spouted, the opalescent vapors rising into the air.

Tomo-chi-chi stood at the bow with Tooanahowie,

42

watching until the mists disappeared and the great whales had gone. Evening feathered the edges of the sky and the sea was rose-colored and stippled. Looking out to where the whales had been, Tomo-chi-chi said, "I've never seen such a wondrous sight."

The journey to England took seventy days. In a letter to his friend, Sir John Phillips, announcing their arrival in London, Oglethorpe wrote:

An aged chief named Tomo-chi-chi, the *mico* or king of Yamacraw, a man of excellent understanding, is so desirous of having the young people taught the English language, that notwithstanding his advanced age, he has come over with me to obtain means. He has brought with him a young man whom he calls his nephew and next heir, and who has already learned the Lord's Prayer in the English and Indian language. I shall leave the Indians at my estate till I go to the city, where I shall have the happiness to wait upon you, and to relate all things to you more fully, over which you will rejoice and wonder.

*You have carried me through a great many houses to make
me believe that the King's house consisted of many houses.
But I was surprised to find I returned by the same stairs I
went up, by which I knew it was still but one house.*

—Tomo-chi-chi

Chapter Nine

THERE WERE OTHER WONDROUS SIGHTS IN
store for the Indians. Not in the same way that the whales
were wondrous, but still exciting. They had never seen as
many people in one place as they saw in London. The
noise and the bustle, the horses and carts, astounded them.
People gathered around to stare and to touch them, and
often strangers came up to them with gifts of flowers and
food. On their tours of London they saw great houses.
They heard bells for the first time—huge bells that tolled
the hours of the day. They watched as barges sailed by on
the Thames and one day saw the Royal Horse Guards pass
in review.

They were entertained at Charlton, the home of Sir
John Persival, one of the Trustees. The house was huge
and surrounded by rolling lawns and an avenue of lime
trees. At dinner, long tables were spread with white
damask cloths. Candles burned in silver candelabra and a
gentleman played the harpsichord, the tinkling music
chiming through the great rooms. Tomo-chi-chi and
Senawki were seated opposite their hosts. Sir John later

44

told his wife how impressed he was with the old *mico's* manners. "He seemed to know that it was polite to wait to take the first mouthful only after their hosts were served." Tomo-chi-chi looked around the great rooms, impressed with their size and luxury, yet not envious. "You English know many things my countrymen do not, but I doubt that you are happier. You live harder than we, and we are more innocent."

Sir John was much taken with Tomo-chi-chi and enjoyed their conversations. He also found it hard to believe that the old *mico* was close to ninety years old. "He looks more like a man of fifty," he later told Oglethorpe.

From Oglethorpe's estate at Godalming, the Indians moved to rooms at Westminster in London. From there, they would visit the king and queen.

Tomo-chi-chi and Senawki dressed carefully for their audience, and wore capes of scarlet and gold. Hillispilli painted his face black and white, and Tooanahowie wore a new English waistcoat of blue embroidered in silver. It had been a gift from Sir John, who had also arranged for a portrait to be painted of Tomo-chi-chi and his adopted son. The other braves were persuaded by Oglethorpe to wear trousers, but they did insist on painting their faces; some half black, others triangular, and others with bearded arrows instead of whiskers.

Three of the king's coaches, each drawn by six fine horses, took the Indians to Kensington Palace to be presented to His Majesty, George II. Everyone went except Stimaulki, who was ill.

At the door of the palace, they were received by the king's bodyguard and then by the Duke of Grafton, who presented them to the king. The great room was filled with people, members of the court and visitors who wanted a glimpse of the Indians. Tomo-chi-chi approached the throne. He walked slowly, his back straight. He was carrying three eagle's feathers.

45

These are the feathers of the eagle which is the swiftest of birds, and who flieth all round our nations. These feathers are a sign of peace in our land, and have been carried from town to town there. We have brought them over to leave with you as a sign of everlasting peace.

After the speeches had ended, Tooanahowie wanted to do something to please the queen, who had been kind to him. He recited the Lord's Prayer in English for her. She was so delighted that she called him over and hugged him. Then the Prince of Wales gave the young boy a fine, gold, pocket watch with a delicate chime.

Later the Georgia delegation was given a tour of the palace. They were impressed with the size of the huge rooms. After walking up the grand staircase and back down again, Tomo-chi-chi said, "You have carried me through a great many houses to make me believe that the king's house consisted of many houses. But I was surprised to find I returned by the same stairs I went up, by which I knew it was still but one house."

When they returned to their rooms at Westminster, they were met with bad news. Stimaulki was stricken with the pox.

Three days later, Tomo-chi-chi stood in a fine, misting rain at St. John's cemetery. Stimaulki was being buried. His body had been sewn into two blankets over a deal board, and lashed together with cord. Only Tomo-chi-chi, three of the other braves, the upper church warden, and the gravediggers were present. People were afraid of the pox, so they stayed away. Tomo-chi-chi had forbidden Senawki and Tooanahowie to attend the burial for fear of the disease.

As the body was lowered into the grave, Tomo-chi-chi handed some of Stimaulki's possessions—beads and silver—to Hillispilli, who then placed them in the grave. Tomo-chi-chi was greatly saddened by the death of his friend and brother-in-law, and by the fact that they were so far from home. It was the first burial of a Native American on British soil.

After the burial, the Indians were invited by Oglethorpe to stay at his home, where they could have the privacy they needed to mourn Stimaulki's death. They remained at Godalming for two weeks.

When the time of mourning had ended, Tomo-chi-chi was invited to meet with the Archbishop of Cantebury. As he entered the rooms at Lambeth, the archbishop, who was quite feeble with age, was supported by two men, one at each elbow. Tomo-chi-chi had looked forward to speaking with him, to exchange ideas on religion. But out of respect for the ailing cleric, who refused to be seated, Tomo-chi-chi kept his greetings brief. Not for anything would he have been discourteous in requiring that the archbishop remain standing for very long. Later, he told Sir John that "I at first believed the archbishop to be a magician because he is so old, and had so much respect from his people." He smiled, then continued, "but then, he was so kind that I knew him to be good." These remarks are interesting when you consider that Tomo-chi-chi was probably older than the archbishop at the time.

Not long after, Tomo-chi-chi paid a visit to Eton, a preparatory school for boys founded by Henry VI in 1440. He spoke to the assembled students and asked the Reverend Dr. George to allow the boys a holiday. The boys were delighted with him, and later showed him through the dark, paneled halls where the names of former students were carved on the walls. Running a long, slender finger over some of the names, Tomo-chi-chi said, "Touching the names brings back the pictures of those named."

The following day, the group visited Hampton Court where they saw the royal apartments, and walked in the gardens where a large group of people had assembled to meet them. Everywhere they went, the Creeks were treated with kindness. If they sometimes tired of people staring at them, their good manners kept them from showing it. They were later taken to the Tower of London, Greewich

Hospital, and all the interesting spectacles in London. Tomo-chi-chi did mention to Oglethorpe that he was surprised that "short-lived men should build such long-lived houses." He evidently missed nothing. His eyes were sharp as was his mind and he noticed everything. At times he seemed oppressed by the poverty he saw. "There are no beggars among my people," he said.

If the passage were by land, we would make nothing of going
on foot though all the way was through woods, and
the night dark as now.

—Tomo-chi-chi

Chapter Ten

IN SEPTEMBER, THERE WAS A MEETING AT
Charleston to discuss business with the Trustees concerning trade agreements between the Creeks and the English.
The earlier treaty signed in the new colony was not always
honored by the whites. The Creeks were paying more than
twice for goods than what the whites were paying. They
were being cheated in the way goods were weighed and
measured. Tomo-chi-chi demanded to know why.

He explained the problems and waited for John
Musgrove to interpret his words. From one end of the long
table in the great hall, he signalled to John to begin. There
was silence. Looking up, Tomo-chi-chi at first thought that
John Musgrove was ill. Perhaps he'd taken the pox. A moment later he realized that the man was drunk. Furious,
Tomo-chi-chi rose and left the room. He was too polite to
criticize John in front of the other men, but he was very,
very angry. "If Mary had come instead, this would not have
happened," he told Sir John.

A few days later, John Musgrove was once again at the
bargaining table, but this time was on his best behavior.
The talks resumed, and the problems of weights and mea-

sures were settled to Tomo-chi-chi's satisfaction. A settlement was made that each town would have only one trader or dealer, licensed, in order that some records could be kept.

Tomo-chi-chi spoke to the Trustees: "Although I have been here but a brief time, I can see that in England nothing is done without money. With us, if we have but two mouthsfull, we give one away."

Sir John later said that "They (the Indians) are so charitable that they can't bear to see another in want, and not give him what he desires, and their houses are always open to strangers."

But expenses were much on the old *mico's* mind. When the business was settled, he announced that it was time for them to return home. At the time, the Indians had been in England nearly four months. But Tomo-chi-chi felt that too much money was being spent on them by the English. "In my own country, travelers are made welcome and entertained without expense."

When the meetings concluded, the English paid John Musgrove 100 pounds sterling for his services as interpreter, but they too, were disgusted by his behavior.

Tomo-chi-chi and Sir John Persival had become good friends over the months. They had begun the custom of taking long walks through the fields and gardens of Charlton, discussing many things. Even though he wanted to go home, Tomo-chi-chi was sad at leaving new-found friends. Yet he felt that he had to go back to his own people. He and Sir John were out walking. In late September, the leaves had turned to bronze and gold and there was a look of winter in the sunlight. "The cold weather is coming," said Tomo-chi-chi, walking in the dappled sunlight. "We need to return home. I know we can only go by ship, but if the passage were by land, we would make nothing of going on foot, though all the way was through woods, and the night dark."

Sir John had brought the old man a gift, which he now

gave him. He handed him a gilt tobacco box. Accepting it, Tomo-chi-chi said, "I will get a ribbon and hang this next to my heart. I came to see you with a good will, and I leave in friendship."

Later, when Tooanahowie saw the box, he was very impressed. He went to Sir John and told him that he had brothers at home and needed to take gifts to each of them. Amused, Sir John said, "And what would you like to take back to these brothers?"

"Guns," replied Tooanahowie promptly. "And I have six brothers so I need six guns."

Before leaving England, Tomo-chi-chi and Senawki arranged to have the furs they had brought with them delivered to the Trustees. In his journal, Sir John made this notation:

> A present received of 25 buckskins,
> One tyger skin
> And six Bouffler skins from Tomo-chi-chi to the Trustees.

Since there were never any tigers in Georgia, the "tyger" skin must have been a wildcat or a panther skin that the Trustees received.

In the *Gentleman's Magazine* from London, October 1734, there appeared the following notice:

> The king, queen, and prince, etc., set out from the Georgia offices in the king's coaches for Gravesend, to embark on their return home. During their stay in England, which has been about four months, His Majesty allowed them 120 a week for their subsistence, and they have been entertained in the most agreeable manner possible. . .They appeared particularly delighted at seeing His Highness perform his exercise of riding the managed horse, the Horse Guards pass in review, and the agreeable appearance of barges, etc., on the Thames on Lord Mayor's Day.

Tomo-chi-chi and the others returned on board the transport ship, *Prince of Wales*. Also on board were 27 English and 57 Salzburgers. After the voyage, Captain Dunbar wrote in his log: "We arrived here in Georgia all cheerful and in good health. The Indians behaved with the accustomed modesty, as did also the Salzburgers, who are a sober and pious people, and gave much less trouble than I expected."

They docked at Savannah on December 27, 1734. James Oglethorpe remained in England, trying to raise monies and troops to protect the new colony from Spain, which threatened war more and more.

*The English are our brothers and friends and we should
protect them against danger and go with them to war
against their enemies.*

—Tomo-chi-chi

Chapter Eleven

BACK IN GEORGIA, TOMO-CHI-CHI GATHERED
together various Creeks and a group of Cherokee chiefs at
Yamacraw for a meeting, and then to see the new town of
Savannah. He told them of his visit to England and about
the long sea voyage. He asked them to continue their
friendship with the English and to observe the obligations
of the new treaties.

"The English are a generous nation," he said. "and will
trade with us on the most honorable and advantageous
terms. They are our brothers and friends and we should
protect them against danger and go with them to war
against their enemies." He then showed them the gifts he
had brought back, in particular the gilt tobacco box from
Sir John, which was his favorite present.

The Indians had made such a good impression in England, and had so awakened the interest of the public, that
Oglethorpe and the Trustees were able to gain sympathy
and support for the new colony. Savannah became a real
place to the general public. They had met the Indians and
were much taken by them.

When his meeting concluded with the Creeks and

Cherokees, Tomo-chi-chi had a letter sent to the Trustees. On the inside of a neatly-dressed buffalo skin, figures were drawn in red and black. Called hide painting, the work gave an account of the history of the Indians, how they came to be on this earth, how they were created out of the earth. When men did the painting, they were usually works showing historical events. Women painted geometric designs, intricate and subtle. The Indians used figures in much the same way that the ancient Egyptians used hieroglyphics, pictures that explained a meaning. The letter also told of the thanks of the Creeks and the Cherokees for the courtesies extended by the English to Tomo-chi-chi and his party. It told, too, of their admiration for James Oglethorpe and the British kingdom. Contained within the drawing was the message: "Some men have more knowledge than others, but let them remember the strong and the weak must one day become dirt alike."

When the Trustees received the skin, they had it framed and placed in the Georgia offices at Westminster.

While Tomo-chi-chi had been away, there were several bad occurences in the town concerning Indians. Although Oglethorpe had forbidden the sale of rum in the colony, there was always someone who would bring it in from Carolina, where spirits were allowed. Two Creek men had been badly beaten and robbed, and one man died after drinking bad rum. Joseph Watson, a dishonest trader and part-time business partner of John Musgrove, had boasted that he would drink to death an Indian warrior. Skea did indeed, drink and die of alcohol poisoning at the hands of Watson. The Creeks were prepared to take the matter into their own hands.

Under the treaty signed in 1733, the Creeks had agreed to abide by the laws of England in matters between the English and Indians. But some of the Creeks wanted revenge and had threatened to kill Watson. Tomo-chi-chi re-

54

minded them of the treaty and suggested that they first see if justice would be done by the English. Upon hearing the complaint, officials in Savannah promised that a warrant would be issued for Watson's arrest. His license for trading with the Indians was revoked and he was locked up until he could be brought to trial. Later he was convicted and punished. Again, violence was averted by Tomo-chi-chi's wisdom and patience.

On an early spring day, Tomo-chi-chi and Hillispilli left the office of the magistrate in Savannah and walked towards the public gardens. They were admiring some of the exotic plants that had been brought from faraway places. As they walked, they saw a man sitting beneath a magnolia tree sketching some of the plants. Tomo-chi-chi greeted Baron von Reck politely and admired his work. The baron, who had arrived in the colony earlier, had come to greet the newest Salzburgers who had arrived on board the *Prince of Wales* with Tomo-chi-chi. Since they didn't speak the same language, a conversation was difficult, but Tomo-chi-chi admired the baron's sketches and invited him to walk through the gardens with them.

As they approached the town square, a group of children, mostly English boys, had gathered. Their screams and laughter sounded loud and shrill. The men exchanged glances; something was wrong. As they drew near, they saw that a crocodile had been captured and was slowly being beaten to death by the boys. They were throwing rocks and sticks and a few, braver than the rest, were hitting the animal with clubs. The animal had been captured and put on display so that the newcomers to the colony wouldn't be afraid of the creatures that had been described to them as "terrible to look at, big enough to swallow a man, with rows of dreadful sharp teeth. Feet like a dragon's, armed with great claws and a long tail which they throw about."

Baron von Reck began sketching the animal. Tomo-chi-

chi whispered something to Hillispilli and they soon left. At nightfall, when the watchman arrived to check the square, he found the crocodile mercifully dead. It had been killed neatly and swiftly.

Tomo-chi-chi's dream was finally about to come true. He ordered the construction of the school he had planned for so long. He chose as the site the ancient burial mounds of his people. The school, which was named the *Irene,* was built of clay and clapboard. Its outer walls were smooth and thick, and the inner walls were covered with boards of fragrant *wisso*. Long benches lined the walls and were covered with soft furs. In a place of honor hung a portrait of James Oglethorpe. There was also picture of the Great Lion of England, which had been a gift from the Trustees after Tomo-chi-chi admired a similar painting at the Tower of London.

When the school was finished, Tomo-chi-chi invited Chigelley, Malatchi, and some of the other Creek *micos* to a dedication ceremony. When Chigelley saw the school where the Indian children would be taught, he was very pleased. The children would learn to read the "talking leaves." He told Tomo-chi-chi that "Perhaps the time is now come when all our children are to be taught learning."

Malatchi added, "If I had twenty children, I would have them all taught." When the school was opened, Mary Musgrove helped in teaching the children to read and write. Then her husband, John Musgrove, died, and she was needed to help at Mount Venture.

In England, Oglethorpe resumed his seat in Parliament. He secured the passage of two bills. One was the act to prohibit the importation and sale of rum, brandy, and other distilled liquors within the limits of Georgia. The other bill forbade the introduction of slavery into the colony. Both of these bills received royal sanction. It was now law: there would be no rum and there would be no slavery in the royal colony of Georgia.

More ships and settlers began arriving in the new colony. South of Savannah, the village of Highgate was laid out and settled by twelve French families. And to the east, the village of Hampstead was settled by twelve German families. A small fort was built with mounted cannon at Thunderbolt. Captain McPherson and a party of Rangers had been stationed just above Yamacraw Bluff on a point on the river known as the Horse Quarter. At this time, the government was gravely concerned about the danger to the new colony from the French who had settlements along the Mississippi River. Oglethorpe was concerned about the Spaniards and proposed to build two forts of eighty men and eighteen forts of forty men along the southern borders.

That same year, the Trustees commissioned Lt. Hugh Mackay to recruit volunteers from among the Highlanders of Scotland. One hundred and thirty men, and fifty women and children were enrolled at Inverness to leave for Savannah. They sailed on October 18, 1735 on board the *Prince of Wales,* commanded by Captain George Dunbar. These people proved to be a valuable asset to the colony. They were not reckless adventurers or exiled by poverty or debts. They were hand-picked men, chosen for their military qualities. Coming primarily from the glen of Stralbdean, they were accompanied on the journey by their own minister, the Reverend John McLeod.

A few days after their arrival at Savannah, they were transported in piraguas up the Altamaha River to a point about 16 miles above St. Simon's Island. There, they formed a permanent settlement called New Inverness. To the district they were to hold and cultivate, they gave the name Darien.

In a short time, Tomo-chi-chi and his men were working with the Scots to construct a road connecting New Inverness with Savannah. The Creeks and the Highlanders became good friends.

White men know much, yet they build great houses as if
they were going to live forever. But white men cannot
live forever. In a little time, white men will be dust as
well as I.

—Tomo-chi-chi

Chapter Twelve

OGLETHORPE RETURNED TO SAVANNAH FROM England on February 5, 1736, on board the *Symond,* one of two ships that left on what was called "the Grand Embarkation." Two vessels had been charted by the Trustees, the *Symond* and the *London Merchant.* Among the stores on board were cannon, small arms, ammunition, and large quantities of provisions. As a convoy, H.M.S. *Hawk,* a sloop of war, was detailed to accompany the ships.

Among the passengers on board the *Symond* was a young English preacher named John Wesley, who had been appointed as resident minister in Georgia. His brother, Charles Wesley, wanted to accompany him, and was accepted by Oglethorpe as his private secretary. Charles was also given the position as secretary to Indian affairs in the province of Georgia. So it was that John Wesley was on his way to the new colony to convert the Indians to Christianity, while Charles would be giving advice on a subject of which he knew next to nothing. It would not turn out well for either man. John Wesley had no idea just how he was going to accomplish the conversion, and he evidently never questioned whether the Indians wanted to be converted. As Charles Jones said in his *History of Georgia*, "If sage counsel had been observed, the Rev. Mr. John Wesley would have been spared no little annoyance and mortification during his residence in Georgia. And the community in Savannah would have escaped much which engendered ill-will and distraction."

Upon reaching Savannah, Wesley's first request was to meet with Tomo-chi-chi. Oglethorpe arranged the meeting and called upon Mary Musgrove to help as interpreter, since Wesley knew none of the Indian languages.

Tomo-chi-chi, Senawki, Tooanahowie, and Mary Musgrove came to greet the young preacher. Senawki brought fresh milk and honey as a gift to him. The morning was bright and cold, the wind out of the northeast and brisk. Brown pelicans skimmed the top of the water and the ship creaked at anchor. Both Mary and Senawki were wrapped in woolen shawls while Tomo-chi-chi wore a supple deer-skin over his shoulders.

With exquisite courtesy, Tomo-chi-chi welcomed the young man. When the introductions were complete and everyone was seated, John Wesley began to question the old *mico* about religion.

"What do you think you were made for?" asked Wesley.

"He that is above knows what He made us for," replied Tomo-chi-chi, "We know nothing. We are in the dark." He settled back and lit his clay pipe. The smoke was fragrant and encircled his head. Mary and Senawki exchanged glances. This would be interesting. Tomo-chi-chi loved talking with the English about any subject. This man was young, but it still might be interesting.

Wesley smiled, obviously pleased at the old man's answer.

"White men know much," said Tomo-chi-chi, "yet they build great houses as if they were going to live forever. But white men cannot live forever. In a little time, white men will be dust as well as I."

59

Senawki poured out cups of milk and honey and passed them around the room. Thanking her, Wesley said, "We have a large book that teaches that men should not build up treasures on earth."

"Indians do not," said Tomo-chi-chi. "Only white men do that."

The two men talked for a long time. Sometimes the others joined in the conversation, but after awhile Tomo-chi-chi grew annoyed. It was as though the sacred beliefs of his own people counted for nothing. He tried to explain to the young preacher that so far the Indians were not very impressed with some of the things they had seen Christians do. Besides, he asked. "Why do all men have to be Christians? Why aren't the Grandfathers and the Great Spirit of our people respected by the whites?"

Wesley shrugged off these questions. "Why don't your people convert to Christianity?" he asked.

"Because," said the old *mico*. "We have seen these Christians! These are Christians at Savannah! Christians at Frederica! These Christians get drunk! Beat men and tell lies! No, I tell you, I am no Christian!"

In an effort to make peace, Wesley began asking more politely about Indian beliefs. "Do you often think and talk of your Beloved Ones?"

"We think of them always, wherever we are. We talk of them and to them, at home and abroad, in peace, in war, before and after we fight. And indeed, whenever and wherever we meet together," replied Tomo-chi-chi, a bit more calmly.

Unfortunately, Wesley didn't take the counsel of his former teacher, the Rev. Dr. Burton, who had advised him to "Keep in view the pattern of St. Paul, who became all things to all men that he might gain some." Wesley never learned the Muskogean language so it was almost impossible for him to fully communicate with the Indians in a meaningful way. In the end, he devoted himself to work among the settlers. Later, he began classes for children, creating the first Sunday schools in the colony. Before he returned to England, he founded the Methodist Episcopal Church in the new world.

In March, Tomo-chi-chi and Oglethorpe left Savannah with a scouting party of forty Creek braves for the offshore islands. The scouting party was on its way to Darien, where it would meet up with a company of thirty Highlanders under the command of Captain Hugh Mackay. The expedition was, according to Oglethorpe's diary, to "see where his Majesty's Dominions and the Spaniards joined." At the time, the southernmost islands were claimed by both countries.

The scout boats darted like dragonflies over twisting inlets and waterways of the islands that for centuries had been unexplored and uninhabited. Herons and sandhill cranes watched from the marshes as the boats passed. A racoon, his bandit face curious, darted into the brush. Alligator nests, like low tents, were built along the water's edge. As the boats approached, one of the great beasts would waddle into the water, leaving a wake behind him.

The men passed swamps where cypress trees cast feathery shadows on the trembling earth. Their branches were alive with birds. Flocks of parakeets, bright as jewels, swooped from one tree to another. Tomo-chi-chi told Oglethorpe that the birds fed on the seeds of the cypress and nested in the hollows of the trunks during the cold months.

From Darien, the combined force proceeded to Cumberland Island, where Fort St. Andrew was established. There, a party of ten Highlanders and ten Creeks remained. The rest of the party, including Tomo-chi-chi, Tooanahowie and Oglethorpe, left for Amelia Island.

The party of Highlanders and Creeks traveled 200 miles, never seeing another human being. They sloshed through seemingly endless twisting canals that wound through miles of marsh into the heart of Spanish-held territory. At night they rested under open skies. When it rained, as it did frequently along the coast, they fashioned rough shelters of boughs and palmetto branches.

Finally, they came to the island that Oglethorpe named *Amelia*, "It being a beautiful Island, the seashore covered with myrtle, peach trees, orange trees, and vines in the wild woods." When they reached the mouth of the St. John's River, where there was a post occupied by Spanish guards, Oglethorpe had to restrain Tomo-chi-chi from ordering his men to make a night attack on the post. They were on a scouting party, and would have to return without being seen. The expedition then continued south toward lands claimed by the Spanish.

After viewing the southernmost lands, Oglethorpe told Tomo-chi-chi that he feared war with Spain was close. He asked the old *mico* for his help should war break out. Tomo-chi-chi pledged his help and that of his people.

Oglethorpe had chosen Frederica as his military base. There a battery of cannon was mounted, ditches dug and a rampart raised and covered with earth. Smoke drifted out to sea as the tall grasses were burned off. The island became a fortress in the wilderness of swamp and marsh. Buildings were constructed of *tabby*, a mixture of shells, lime and sand.

In May, Oglethorpe asked Tomo-chi-chi to supply the troops he'd promised. A party of Spanish commissioners would be visiting Frederica. Oglethorpe wanted them to believe that the new colony and its outlying forts were well defended against attack. A plan was worked out to reinforce the forts along the coast, and defending them were some strange-looking soldiers.

Had I been here, it would not have happened.

—Tomo-chi-chi

Chapter Thirteen

The LIGHT GLINTED AND SPARKLED ON THE water as the piragua, carrying Oglethorpe and his small party, moved lightly toward the white shores of St. Simon's Island. A heavy fog blanketed the coast. The sun shining through the mist was a white ball. The June morning was already hot. Offshore, the British sloop *Hawk* rode at anchor. Aboard were the Spanish commissioners.

Oglethorpe had made his decision to greet them at St. Simon's rather than Frederica. He didn't want them to see the small and still ill-prepared fort. He waited off the coast to greet the visitors. He had only seven men with him, but had arranged with Tomo-chi-chi and Malatchi to have a backup of Creek warriors should they be needed. There was also a party of "some of the genteelest" Highlanders in bright and colorful plaid tartans with swords and claymores that shone in the sun. Oglethorpe intended a good show for his guests. He planned to present the strongest, best-looking Creek warriors, the boldest Highlanders, and his own mounted guard to greet them.

At the time of the presentation, volleys would be fired with orders of "fire, reload, and fire again" given to make it appear that there were far more troops than there actually were. He hoped for the effect of the sound carrying over water and echoing back to produce a grand show of strength.

The Spaniards had been warned that the area was filled with angry Indians, and only with great difficulty were they being restrained from attacking the ship. The *Hawk* moved slowly up the river. On board, the men strained to see the forts through the heavy fog. They could see only vague outlines of soldiers posted along the route.

Suddenly, cannons exploded sharply. The smell of gunpowder drifted out to them at sea. Guns were fired into the air and arrows flew through the air like birds. It appeared that hundreds of troops were defending the fort. The Spaniards couldn't understand it. They had been told that the English were short of troops and the forts practically deserted.

What they couldn't see was that inside the forts, the men were dashing from one side to the other, firing, then dashing to another spot to fire again. One young Highlander ran from one cannon to another doing all the firing himself. The Creeks shouted war whoops and shot their weapons into the air.

The show was a complete success. When the ship was out of sight, the men began slapping one another on the back, laughing and cheering. Then they went around collecting the "extra" soldiers from the fields and marshes. They had stuck sticks into the ground with cross pieces, and then draped coats and caps over them. An army of scarecrows had worked. The truth was that less than 100 men—including Rangers, Creeks, Highlanders and guard—had made up the army.

On the morning of June 18, 1736, Oglethorpe and seven of his men were rowed out to the *Hawk*. He presented himself to the Spanish commissioners as His Majesty's representative. Nearby, a man-of-war was moored. Assembled on deck were Highlanders. On the opposite side, a detachment of independent companies in regimentals stood at attention. Spanish sailors manned the shrouds and kept sentry with drawn cutlasses at the cabin door.

After dinner, the Spanish commissioners drank to the health of King George II and the royal family. Then they toasted the health of the king and queen of Spain. Cannons were fired and were answered by heavy fire from the island. Presents of snuff, chocolates, and wine were made by the commissioners. In return, they were given gifts of butter, cheese, fresh meat, and fruit.

Then, Malatchi, Tomo-chi-chi, and Hillispilli, in full war dress, leading thirty warriors also in war dress, boarded the *Hawk*. They entered the captain's cabin silently and stood unmoving. Stunned, the commissioners watched. The tension in the cabin was strong, the very walls seemed to contain anger that rose and fell in waves. Then Hillispilli stepped forward.

Demanding justice for past outrages against his people, he spoke eloquently. Both commissioners, Montiano and Don Pedro, grew alarmed. From where he sat opposite them, Oglethorpe remained cool and calm. He gave the impression that only his power over the Indians kept them in control. Then he spoke, as had been arranged earlier between himself and the Indians.

"Present these complaints to your governor," he told the commissioners. "These men are loyal subjects of the Crown and demand satisfaction."

Then Tomo-chi-chi stepped forward. His timeless face was worthy of respect as he told of a brutal massacre committed by the Spaniards against the Creeks. "When this thing happened, we were gone with Colonel Oglethorpe to England. Had I been here, it would not have happened. For if I had been with my men, they would not have been surprised. All the chiefs were in England with the English instead of on their own lands where they belonged!" Furious, the cords in his neck stood out like ropes as he waited for the translator to interpret his words to the commissioners.

65

When they understood, they made a motion to be allowed to speak, but Hillispilli spoke. "Now," he said, "we will go and find our enemies and kill them. You will go with me and you shall see how I punish them. But if you will not help me, I have many friends, enough who will go with me to revenge this murder." The Creeks shouted approval and the noise in the cabin was deafening.

Don Pedro rose and addressed the Creeks. "The man's name who is guilty of this crime is Pohoia, the king of the Floridas. It was he who ordered the crimes. I promise that the Spanish Governor will secure him and punish him for his crimes."

Then Malatchi said, "If we see this thing done, *then* we will believe you."

Tomo-chi-chi had grown somewhat calmer and after whispered words with Oglethorpe, persuaded Hillispilli and the others to maintain control. He talked them out of violence, telling them that it was a manner of honor that they remain calm. "Colonel Oglethorpe has invited us here, and we cannot strike a man in another man's home."

The conference resulted in a temporary peace, which lasted about two years. The Treaty of Frederica followed, in which it was agreed that neither Spain nor England would occupy the mouth of the St. John's River. But soon the Spaniards would order the English to leave Georgia. Then, war was certain.

Once again, Oglethorpe left for England. He narrowly escaped shipwreck in the Bristol Channel, but reached London in early January, 1737. Once there, he petitioned the Crown for a "necessary supply of forces" to protect the colony. That same year, when he was forty-eight years old, Oglethorpe was named colonel of a new regiment of soldiers consisting of six companies of 100 each, exclusive of musicians and non-commissioned officers. He was also appointed general and Commander-in-chief of His Majesty's forces in Carolina and Georgia.

On a bright September morning in 1738, Oglethorpe and his convoy had arrived at Jekyl Sound. With him were 700 men, women and children in five transports convoyed by the men-of-war, *Blandford* and *Hector*. The troops landed on the south end of St. Simon's Island. From the battery came the salute, the shots echoing over the wide beaches, the faint smoke drifting into the horizon.

At Yamacraw, Tomo-chi-chi received word that his friend Oglethorpe had returned from England. On the 8th of October, General Oglethorpe, along with Captain Hugh Mackay and Captain Sutherland, set out in an open boat for Savannah. Tomo-chi-chi knew of his arrival even before the piragua was sighted by the townspeople. As the small boat came into view of the bluffs, the militia saluted the general with cannon fire. Bonfires were built along the shore and there was an all-night celebration.

The following day, Tomo-chi-chi got up from his sick-bed, where he had lain ill for nearly a month. Insisting that he was now well, he went into town to call upon his old friend. The October morning was golden, and the dry, dusty scent of oak leaves scented the air.

Tomo-chi-chi was welcomed to Oglethorpe's small house overlooking the river. They greeted one another and Tomo-chi-chi told Oglethorpe that, "I am so glad to see you that it makes me moult like an eagle." He also told him that several of the chiefs of the Creek nation were at his lodge, waiting to present their congratulations upon his safe arrival and to assure him of their loyalty to the king. Oglethorpe invited them to his home and on the 13th, Tomo-chi-chi accompanied them back to Savannah.

At the appointed time, four chiefs of various tribes, and thirty warriors with fifty-two attendants came down the river from Yamacraw. As they landed and walked up the bluff at Savannah, they were saluted by a battery of cannon and escorted by a detachment of militia to the town hall where General Oglethorpe was waiting. After offering their congratulations, the Indians told him that not long before, the Spaniards had invited them to St. Augustine under the pretense that they would meet Oglethorpe there. When they discovered that he was not, the Creeks were told that he was ill and on board a ship in the harbor. Disgusted at being lied to, the Creeks returned to Georgia. To Oglethorpe, they promised their support and offered to send 1,000 warriors subject to his command.

An invitation was extended to Oglethorpe to visit their towns which he promised to do. That night, there was a party and celebration at Yamacraw at which the general was present. The next morning, the Creeks left for their respective homes.

Oglethorpe was furious that the Creeks had been lied to by the Spaniards. Yet, he was honored that the Creeks were so loyal to him. Not long after this, Oglethorpe accepted an invitation to a *puskita,* where he would meet with them again.

*As soon as ever the Ground was found and fit to stand
upon, it came to us, and has been with us ever since.*

—Postubee, a Holy Man

Chapter Fourteen

THE YEAR 1739 WAS HERALDED BY SUNSPOTS. There were thunderstorms and winds from the sea, and a waterspout moved up the Savannah River. Colored lightning—pink, blue, and lavender—was seen in the hills. A Cherokee chief reported that in his village a ball of lightning rolled down the chimney and across the floor of a cabin. Many thought the lightning was an omen, but whether good or bad remained to be seen.

In July, Oglethorpe wrote in his journal: "I am still embarrassed by the many violations of the Rum Law, and the settlers still pester me for slaves. . . I wish I could make the people see what harm can come from owning slaves. Yet, only the Highlanders and the Salzburgers support me in this."

And on July 17, he wrote: "*The James* sailed for England with twenty pounds weight of silk. We had hoped for more, but many worms died. They were being bred in a house formerly used as a hospital. Mr. Camuse believes that the infections inherent in the building caused the sickness that killed them. We have moved them and built a new house for them."

When the silk was received in London, it was woven by

the firm of Thomas Lomb. A bolt was then sent to the queen who said it was the finest she'd ever seen. Another bolt was sent to Mary Musgrove.

In the meantime, Oglethorpe had ordered that stockades be built and cannon added to the defense of Savannah. The Yamassee Indians were crafty allies of the Spaniards, and as elusive as quicksilver. Sudden fires and night raids were their specialty, and Oglethorpe was particularly concerned about Mount Venture. It was still unmanned and vulnerable. He sent a small party to reinforce it, and requested that Mary Musgrove return to her home in town where she'd be safe.

The time for the *puskita*, which was to be held at Coweta, was approaching. The four great Indian nations of the Southeast would meet—the Creeks, Cherokees, Choctaws, and Chickasaws. More than 7000 people were expected to take part in the Green Corn Festival.

At his house in town on St. Simon's Island, Oglethorpe sat in front of the fire. He held a bundle of slender tapers in his hand. Malatchi had given them to him.

"Throw away one stick a day," he'd said, "and when you reach the final one, you will have time to travel to Coweta for the meeting."

Tomo-chi-chi, too, wanted to attend the meeting. The old *mico* was eighty-nine years old. The night before, as he lay in his lodge, he had heard an owl call his name. It was close to his time and he knew it. He'd hoped to make the journey to Coweta but knew that it was not possible. It was there that Tooanahowie would officially take his place as *mico* of the Yamacraws.

Lying on his couch at the lodge, he beckoned to Tooanahowie. With eyes grown dim with age, he watched as Toonahowie approached. He was tall and handsome with pleasant features and fine eyes. He had given Tomo-chi-chi much joy in his sixteen years. He listened as Tomo-chi-chi explained that he would not be able to make the trip to Coweta.

It had been a strange year. There were ill feelings among some of the Creeks toward the English. Even after all the treaties and promises, there were still some traders who cheated the Creeks and went unpunished. He wanted Tooanahowie to counsel the people that Oglethorpe was always to be trusted. He had always honored his word.

"I will wait for your return," he said, and closed his eyes to rest. Senawki came into the lodge with a gourd filled with cool water for him. She told Tooanahowie goodbye and wished him well on his journey. Then she went to sit at Tomo-chi-chi's side. She, too, knew the time was approaching when her beloved husband would no longer be with her.

"Do you remember when I told you about the cranes?" he asked. "About one man coming to this place and another leaving?"

Senawki nodded. "I remember," she said.

"The second man is myself," Tomo-chi-chi said softly.

The Savannah delegation left for Coweta. Among them were General Oglethorpe, Mary Musgrove, Tooanahowie, four of Oglethorpe's young officers, and four Creek braves. They traveled 300 miles through the forests, crossing streams and rivers, fighting mosquitoes and gnats and watching out for snakes and animals. Occasionally they would find baskets of food that had been left for them: honey, milk, pumpkin bread, venison, corn pudding and dried fruit pies. All along their way, Creek women saw to it that there was food. Sometimes the travelers saw the women but most often only the food would be there, at a crossing or along the side of a stream, to help them on their way.

Holding the sacred tobacco in his left hand, Postubee faced the rising sun. He recited the ancient powerful words and blew his breath on the leaves, while rubbing them with his right hand. The morning sun touched his face and turned it to bronze. The sun gilded the edges of the leaves in the forest around him and danced off the water in the creek in front of him. He rubbed the leaves counter-clockwise. It was good medicine that he had prepared, medicine for the meeting that would take place later in the day at the lodge. Finally, Postubee was ready.

Only Postubee or one of the other holy men was allowed to smoke the sacred tobacco. The custom of sacred tobacco was older than the memory of any person there. Not even the fathers of the old men could remember where the ritual had begun. Like the use of the pipe itself, it had begun when men first came to the places from the beyond, from the lands shrouded by fog and lost in the mists of time. Ancient men had walked to the frozen lands of the north to obtain the sacred stone for the pipes. It took a year for them to walk to the secret caves and to return. And only the holy ones knew where the caves were and what mysteries they held. This would be a good *puskita*, Postubee thought. The omens were right.

Oglethorpe and Tooanahowie were given a warm welcome at Coweta. Chigelley and Malatchi rode out to meet them and to lead them back to the village. The pipe of peace was smoked and then food was prepared. Chigelley announced that he, too, was turning over the reins of power. Malatchi would now be chief *mico* of the Upper and Lower Creek Nation. Tooanahowie would take Tomo-chi-chi's place as chief *mico* of the Yamacraw.

The festival lasted for a week after which Mary Musgrove and the Creeks returned to Savannah. Oglethorpe and his party went on to Fort Moore at Augusta on business. He had planned to spend a week there, but was stricken with a fever and lay on his cot, ill and racked with a sickness that left him drenched with sweat or freezing. His second week there, a party of Cherokees and Chickasaws came to see him. They were complaining that the English had been sell-

72

ing bad rum to their people. They described the results of the poisoning and demanded justice.

"The young men look in the streams and kill themselves. They are scarred and disfigured."

Oglethorpe was dismayed at what he heard. He recognized the symptoms of smallpox. "The traders may have been selling bad rum, but that's not what is killing your people," he said. The Cherokees and Chickasaws had been stricken with the "white man's disease." He assured them that the Georgia traders were licensed and safe and that he would see to it that the bad trader was caught and punished. They thanked him and offered to prepare a potion to cure his illness.

As he drank the bitter, dark brew, Oglethorpe wondered if he was going to die. A little while later, Lt. Mackay came into the room with a message from the governor of Rhode Island. Rewards were being offered for privateers who volunteered to act against Spanish ships. If he understood the message correctly, Oglethorpe knew that it could only mean one thing. War.

"Prepare to leave for Savannah," he said, getting up from his cot. Oddly enough, once his knees stopped shaking, he felt well enough to travel. The Cherokee potion had cured him, at least temporarily. He was weak and had lost weight, but the fever was gone.

Not far from Savannah, a runner met Oglethorpe's party with two urgent messages. England had declared war against Spain. And his old friend Tomo-chi-chi lay dying.

He shall return no more to his house, neither shall
his place know him any more.

—Job 7:10

Chapter Fifteen

THE FIRST LIGHT OF DAY SHONE PALE AND soft in the east. The lodge house was wreathed in silvery river mists that hid the hollows and houses. It seemed as though the village had been enchanted by a magician's wand, so that it floated upon the earth. The breeze was gentle and smelled of the sea. An owl drifted silently through the trees, the rounded tips of his feathers masking all sound. The day was October 5, 1739.

Tomo-chi-chi lay on a raised bed of furs in the center of the room. Firelight flickered over his face, turning to gold his hooded eyelids, and shadowing the fragile hollows at his temples. His hands, twisted and arthritic, held the gilt box given to him by Sir John Persival. From a dark corner of the room came the sound of a drum, as muffled as a heartbeat.

Rows of people stood silently along the walls. At the foot of the bed, Tooanahowie kept watch. Senawki and Mary Musgrove sat on either side of the bed.

"Tomo-chi-chi," Mary whispered. "Can you hear me?"

Tomo-chi-chi's heavy eyelids fluttered, reluctant to open.

"Coosaponakeesa, it is you." His voice was whispery and thin. He opened his eyes slowly and turned his head

74

toward her. "I have been waiting for my friend, the general."

"He is on his way," she said, placing her warm hand over his cool, knotted one.

But she didn't know whether he heard her. Tomo-chi-chi's eyes closed and he died.

The day of the funeral was cool and golden. Autumn leaves lay with the elegance of crushed silk along the paths. James Oglethorpe stood on the banks of the river, watching the funeral barge bearing the body of Tomo-chi-chi glide silently on the jade-green water. Ever-widening circles floated out from the barge and touched the banks where people watched and waited.

When the barge reached its destination, the pallbearers, Oglethorpe among them, lifted their burden and bore the wrapped body on its stretcher down Bay Street. They turned at Bull Street and then walked south toward Persival Square, where the old *mico* would be buried. It had been his wish that he be buried in the square of the town that he had helped to settle. Tooanahowie, Senawki, and Mary followed directly behind the pallbearers. Following them were the *micos*, chiefs and braves representing the various tribes of the Nation. Only the singing of birds and the slow, steady footfalls of the mourners disturbed the morning's silence.

As they approached the square, minute guns were fired into the air by the militia. The shots shattered the stillness, and reverberated in the air. A few minutes later, the body was lowered into the earth. Suddenly, as though on signal, a cloud of sandhill cranes flew overhead, their feathers creaking as they sailed low over the square. The great birds rippled and soared, filling the hollowed air with their flight, filling the emptiness. Mary watched until the cranes disappeared over the river.

"*In my dream, the cranes flew twice*," Tomo-chi-chi had

said that day at St. Catherine's Island. *"Once to tell me of a man who is to come and once to tell me of a man who is no more on this earth."* Mary remembered his words.

All through the long years, she would remember Tomochi-chi with love. He had been good to her. She remembered when her baby had died, newly-born. Tomo-chi-chi had come to see her.

"He has taken the path of light," he'd said, gently and sweetly.

"And now you have taken the path of light," she said, watching the cranes fly away.

*When we call into remembrance the then force of these
tribes. . .surely we may proudly ask, what soldier
ever gave higher proof of courage?*

—Hon. Thomas Spalding
Collections of the Georgia
Historical Society

Chapter Sixteen

ON AMELIA ISLAND, THE SOUTHERNMOST
outpost of the colony, John Mackay and Angus Mcleod,
two young Highlanders, walked down a narrow path in the
predawn chill to gather firewood. At the fort, the rest of
the small garrison was asleep. As the two men entered the
woods, a volley of shot cut them down without warning.
Within minutes, their heads had been cut off by a war
party of Spanish-allied Yamassee Indians.

November 7, 1739. "*First blood spilt by the hands of the
Spaniard.*" Oglethorpe wrote the words with his quill pen,
then folded the letter carefully. Holding the sealing wax to
the candle, he sealed the letter, pressing his seal into the
soft wax, then dusting the paper lightly with sand.

In December, he wrote to Mary Musgrove:

We are here resolved to die hard and will not lose one inch
of ground without fighting! But we cannot do the impossible. We have no cannon, very little powder, no horses,
very few boats, and no funds. The best expedient I can

77

think of is to strike first. I think the best way to make use of our strength is to use our men, beat (the Spaniards) out of the field, destroy their out-settlements. The Indians, who are very faithful, will assist us. I am fortifying the town of Frederica, and I hope I shall be repaid the expenses. I cannot leave a number of good houses and merchants' goods, and what is much more valuable, the lives of men, women and children in an open town, at the mercy of every party!

Mary promptly sent him 200 pounds sterling, what gunpowder she could spare, and extra weapons from the supply at Mount Venture. The Charles Town legislature agreed to send a regiment of 500 men, a troop of Rangers, and three months' provisions. A large schooner was also furnished.

Oglethorpe then wrote to the Trustees in England: "We desperately need four ten-oared boats and one at Savannah, as well as a train of artillery, some gunners, and at least 400 barrels of cannon and 100 barrels of musket powder, with bullets proportionable."

By now, most of the men in Savannah and surrounding areas, including indentured servants, had been drafted into military service. Mount Venture was now Fort Mount Venture, a military fort. The colony was at war.

In July 1742, the Spaniards stood off St. Simon's Island with 50 vessels, 1,800 soldiers, and some 1,000 sailors. They landed a few miles from Frederica. On July 7th, the Battle of Bloody Marsh began. Marching and countermarching up the road that cut through the center of the island from Fort St. Simon to Frederica, the battle raged. Oglethorpe was at the head of his rangers and Highlanders with Lt. Mackay, and Tooanahowie led the Creeks.

Although Bloody Marsh was considered a minor battle, it was a turning point in the war. Tooanahowie, wounded in the right hand, began using his left hand for firing, and led his men to victory. He was eighteen years old.

The long struggle ended in March 1743 when General Oglethorpe—with a small band of Creek warriors, a detachment of Highlanders, and a portion of his regiment—landed in Florida and drove the enemy within the lines of St. Augustine. They compelled the Spaniards to abandon their advanced posts in Florida. Oglethorpe's troops then marched 96 miles in four days. This was the last expedition led by Oglethorpe against Spain. The war, which began in St. Augustine in defeat for the British, was finally won.

The governors of New York, New Jersey, Pennsylvania, Maryland, and Virginia sent special letters of congratulations to Oglethorpe, thanking him for his services. The Governor of South Carolina did not join in the congratulations, but the people of Port Royal did.

After the war, Oglethorpe returned to Orange Cottage, the home that he had built on St. Simon's, leaving Colonel William Stephens as deputy general of the colony. For months, Oglethorpe and his men were busy rebuilding the settlements at St. Simon's, Cumberland, and Jekyl Island. By 1743, the colony was well established. The Creeks and the English lived together peacefully, and the Spaniards had left the area.

In July, Oglethorpe planned a trip to England. He was greatly in debt because of the war. Some of the bills that he had drawn "for His Majesty's Service" had been returned dishonored in the amount of 12,000 pounds. He needed to get his affairs in order. He left Savannah on July 23,1743. He never returned to the colony.

In England he was commissioned as general in the British Army. He returned to Parliament until 1754. Recognized as governor of the colony until 1752, he maintained an interest and love for Georgia. He married Elizabeth Stanhope in England. When he was ninety years

General James Oglethorpe. Georgia Historical Society.

old, he was introduced to a young woman who was visiting London and who described him as perhaps "the most remarkable man of his time. . .a *preux chevalier*, heroic, romantic, and full of the old gallantry."

A short time before his death, Oglethorpe paid a visit to John Adams, the first minister of the United States of America to the Court of St. James's. The man who, with his friend Tomo-chi-chi, had created the colony of Georgia, met with the man who had come to England as a representative of the country that had declared its separate national existence.

James Edward Oglethorpe died on July 1, 1785, and was buried at Cranham Church in the ancient town of Godalming.

Shortly after Oglethorpe left Savannah for England, Tooanahowie and four other young braves were cutting timber near the edge of town . Without warning, they were attacked by a renegade war party of 43 Yamassee Indians. They were kidnapped and held prisoner aboard a piragua. When word got out, a rescue party of Creeks went after them. They caught up with the Yamassees on the northern side of the St. John's River. During the fight, five Yamasee were killed, as was Tooanahowie. He was twenty one years old. One of the men brought back the gold watch that Tooanahowie had been given by the Prince of Wales on his visit to London. The watch was given to Mary Musgrove, who in turn gave it to Senawki, Tooanahowie's mother. One month later, Senawki died.

Mary Musgrove married again and was widowed during the war. Under English law, most of her lands were taken away because at that time, women were not allowed to inherit land in the colony. Even the lands that had been granted to her by Tomo-chi-chi and Malatchi were taken. After a long, legal battle during which she petitioned the Crown for her rights, Mary was awarded full right and title to St. Catherine's Island. Upon her return from England, she went to St. Catherine's where she had built a home. She never again left her beloved island, and is buried there in an unmarked grave.

Afterword

On April 21,1899, a stone was placed over Tomo-chi-chi's grave in Persival (now Wright) Square in Savannah. One hundred and seventy years after his death, he was remembered by the Georgia Society of the Colonial Dames of America with a granite boulder that bears the following inscription:

> *In memory of Tomo-chi-chi*
> *the mico of the Yamacraws,*
> *the companion of Oglethorpe*
> *and the friend and ally*
> *of the Colony of Georgia.*

There are no more Creeks in the "hunting islands" off Georgia's coast. Over time, their lands were taken from them.

In 1838, during the Indian Removal in Georgia, a majority of the remaining Creeks, along with other Southern tribes, lost their homes and lands. The generosity that the Indians showed toward the whites was not returned.

And the places that knew them, know them no more.

Bibliography

Anderson, Barrow, Screven and Waring. *A Pageant of Years*. Spartenburg, S.C.: Reprint Co., 1974.

Corry, John Pitts. *Indian Affairs in Georgia, 1732–1756*. Philadelphia, 1936.

Coulter, E. Merton. *Georgia: A Short History*. Chapel Hill: University of North Carolina Press, 1933.

Cruickshank, Helen G., ed. *John and William Bartram's America: Selections from the Writings of the Philadelphia Naturalists*. New York, 1957.

Harrell, Sara Gordon. *Tomo-chi-chi: The Story of an American Indian*. Minneapolis, Minn.: Dillon Press, 1978.

Hudson, Charles. *The Southeastern Indians*. Knoxville: University of Tennessee Press, 1976.

Ivers, Larry. *British Drums on the Southern Frontier: The Military Colonization of Georgia, 1733-1749*. Chapel Hill: University of North Carolina Press, 1974.

Jones, Charles C., Jr. *The History of Georgia, Vol. 1*. Spartanburg, S.C.: The Reprint Co., 1969.

Kimber, Edward. *A Relation or Journal of a Late Expedition to the Gates of St. Augustine on Florida. Conducted by the Hon. General James Oglethorpe With a Detachment of His Regiment, etc., from Georgia*. Boston: Reprint, 1935.

Kopper, Philip. *The Smithsonian Book of North American Indians*. Washington, D.C.: Smithsonian Books, 1986.

Lovell, Caroline C., *The Golden Isles of Georgia*. Boston: Little, Brown & Co., 1932.

McPherson, Robert G., ed. *The Journal of the Earl of*

Egmont. Athens: University of Georgia Press, 1962.

Swanton, John R. "Early History of the Creek Indians and Their Neighbors." *Bureau of American Ethnology Bulletin,* 73. 1922.

Walters, Anne Lee. *The Spirit of Native America.* San Francisco: Chronicle Books, 1989.